STRATEGIC PARTNERSHIPS IN THE BIBLE

JONATHAN VORCE

Strategic Partnerships in the Bible

Better Together

Copyright © 2024 by Jonathan Vorce

All rights reserved.

First Edition: 2024

Scripture quotations taken from:

The Holy Bible, New International Version® NIV®

Copyright © 1973, 1978, 1984, 2011 by Biblica, Inc.

Used with permission. All rights reserved worldwide.

The Holy Bible, English Standard Version ® ESV

Copyright © 2001 by Crossway, a publishing ministry of

Good News Publishers. Used by permission.

The New King James Version® NKJV®

Scripture taken from the New King James Version®. Copyright © 1982 by Thomas Nelson. Used by permission. All rights reserved.

King James Version (KJV), public domain.

No part of this book may be reproduced, scanned, or distributed in any printed or electronic form without permission. Please do not participate in or encourage piracy of copyrighted materials in violation of the author's rights. Thank you for respecting the hard work of this author.

❦ Created with Vellum

CONTENTS

Introduction	v
1. Abraham and Lot *Family Bonds and Shared Visions*	1
2. Moses and Aaron *United for a Divine Calling*	11
3. Ruth and Naomi *The Power of Commitment*	21
4. David and Jonathan *A Bond of Loyalty*	37
5. Elijah and Elisha *Passing the Mantle*	45
6. Deborah and Barak *There is Strength in Unity*	59
7. Nehemiah and the People of Jerusalem *We're Building a Wall and We Can't Come Down*	71
8. Esther and Mordecai *Courage Under Fire*	85
9. Paul and Barnabas *A Divinely Appointed Partnership*	97
10. Timothy and Paul *The Power of Mentorship*	107
11. Jesus and His Disciples *Fellowship, Discipleship, Mission*	125
12. Jesus and His Church Today *Continuing the Mission through the Great Commission*	141
13. Forging Kingdom Connections *Building Partnerships for Lasting Impacts*	165
14. May I Introduce You to Jesus? *Discovering the Life Changing Joy of Living for Jesus*	181
About the Author	189
Also by Jonathan Vorce	191

INTRODUCTION

STRATEGIC PARTNERSHIPS IN THE BIBLE

Strategic partnerships are the bedrock of fruitful ministry and play a crucial role in fostering community and collaboration. In a rapidly evolving world, church leaders and Christian believers must lean on these powerful alliances more than ever before, as they navigate the complex challenges and opportunities of modern society. This book aims to explore the concept of strategic partnerships within the Bible, examining key examples and teachings that highlight their importance. By providing valuable insights and practical guidance, the book seeks to help you cultivate and sustain these vital relationships in the present day, ensuring that your ministry thrives and reaches its full potential. Through deepening connections with other believers and organizations, we can strengthen our impact and fulfill our shared mission more effectively.

DEFINING STRATEGIC PARTNERSHIPS IN A BIBLICAL CONTEXT

Strategic partnerships are intentional, mutually beneficial alliances designed to achieve a shared vision. In a biblical context, these partnerships transcend mere collaboration; they are divinely orchestrated relationships that fulfill God's greater purpose. They truly embody what we might call "Kingdom Connections." The Scriptures overflow with examples of such alliances, illustrating their profound significance in advancing God's mission on earth.

Historical Examples from the Bible

The Bible offers numerous historical examples of strategic partnerships that played critical roles in accomplishing God's work. One notable example is the partnership between Moses and Aaron. God paired Moses, who was hesitant due to his speech impediment, with Aaron, his eloquent brother, to lead the Israelites out of Egypt. This divine partnership enabled them to complement each other's strengths and weaknesses, leading to the successful liberation of God's people. We will examine this partnership in greater detail later in this book.

Another significant example is the relationship between Paul and Barnabas in the New Testament. Their partnership was instrumental in spreading the Gospel and establishing churches across the Roman Empire. Barnabas's encouragement and support helped Paul, formerly known as Saul, to transition from a persecutor of Christians to one of the most influential Apostles of Christ. We will also examine this partnership in greater detail later.

Contemporary Examples

In contemporary times, strategic partnerships continue to play a pivotal role in ministry. Modern examples include collaborations between churches and non-profit organizations to address social issues such as global evangelization, poverty eradication, educational alliances, fresh water initiatives, provision for orphans and widows, and healthcare. These partnerships leverage the strengths and resources of each entity to create a more significant impact than they could achieve independently.

HOW TO IDENTIFY AND CULTIVATE STRATEGIC PARTNERSHIPS

Identifying and cultivating strategic partnerships require intentional effort and discernment. Here are some practical steps to guide church and ministry leaders:

1. **Pray for Guidance**: Seek God's wisdom and direction in identifying potential partners. Prayer is essential in discerning His will and ensuring that the partnership aligns with His purpose.
2. **Assess Compatibility**: Evaluate whether the potential partner shares similar values, vision,

and mission. A successful partnership thrives on a strong foundation of shared beliefs and goals.
3. **Build Relationships**: Invest time in building genuine relationships with potential partners. Trust and mutual respect are crucial components of any successful partnership.
4. **Define Roles and Responsibilities**: Clearly outline each partner's roles and responsibilities to avoid misunderstandings and ensure smooth collaboration.
5. **Establish Regular Communication**: Maintain open and regular communication to keep the partnership on track and address any issues promptly.

Strategic partnerships bear abundant fruit, leading to transformed lives and strengthened communities. Consider the story of a small church that partnered with a local non-profit organization to provide after-school programs for at-risk youth. Through this partnership, the church utilized its space and volunteers, while the non-profit provided expertise and resources. Together, they created a safe and nurturing environment where young people could thrive academically and spiritually.

An excellent example can be found in a ministry leader who collaborates with other local ministries to tackle homelessness. By uniting their resources and efforts, they could create a shelter that not only provides temporary housing but also offers job training and counseling services. This collaborative initiative would significantly decrease homelessness in their community, alleviate blight, and elevate the quality of life for everyone involved. Families would thrive, businesses would prosper, and together they would showcase the power of unity in Christ.

CHALLENGES AND SOLUTIONS IN MAINTAINING STRATEGIC PARTNERSHIPS

While strategic partnerships are invaluable, they come with their own set of challenges. Common issues include communication breakdowns, differing expectations, and resource constraints. However, addressing these challenges with grace and wisdom can strengthen the partnership and lead to even greater success.

- **Communication Breakdowns**:
- **Solution**: Establish clear communication channels and regular check-ins to ensure everyone is on the same page. Encourage open and honest dialogue to address any concerns promptly.

- **Differing Expectations**:
- **Solution**: Define the partnership's goals, roles, and responsibilities from the outset. Regularly revisit and adjust these expectations as needed to ensure alignment.

- **Resource Constraints**:

- **Solution**: Leverage the unique strengths and resources of each partner to maximize impact. Be creative in finding solutions and seek additional support from the broader community if necessary.

* * *

Strategic partnerships are a powerful tool for advancing God's kingdom and fostering meaningful change in our communities. By understanding their importance, identifying and cultivating potential partners, and addressing challenges with grace, church leaders and ministry heads can build strong alliances that glorify God and serve His people.

As you read this book, may I encourage you to take actionable steps towards building and nurturing strategic partnerships within your ministry. Remember, you are not alone on this journey. Seek God's guidance, lean on the support of your community, and trust in His provision. Together, we can achieve great things for His glory.

ABRAHAM AND LOT

FAMILY BONDS AND SHARED VISIONS

The story of Abraham and Lot is a beautiful testament to the power of family bonds, spiritual calling, and the shared visions that guide us through life's challenges. Abraham, known as Abram in the early years, heard a divine call to leave his homeland, a call that echoed not just in his ears, but resonated deep within his soul. It was a call to venture into the unknown, to embrace faith as he stepped into a promise not yet fully revealed. In this journey, he carried with him not only his personal aspirations but the company of his beloved nephew, Lot, who had lost his father and found in Abraham a father figure—a source of wisdom, protection, and companionship.

As they journeyed together, traversing deserts and mountains, the bond between Abraham and Lot deepened. Their shared vision of prosperity and faith in God's promises fueled their resolve. However, as both families flourished, the blessings they received became a source of challenge. The land they occupied could no longer sustain them both, prompting disputes among their herdsmen. It was a pivotal moment—an opportunity to reflect on what truly mattered. Abraham, with a heart full of generosity and wisdom, proposed a solution rooted in love and respect. He offered Lot the first choice of land, displaying a profound trust in the divine guidance that had brought them this far.

As Lot chose the lush plains of the Jordan, settling near the vibrant city of Sodom, Abraham remained in the less fertile land. This decision, though tinged with sadness, set the stage for new beginnings. Lot's choice, while initially fruitful, led him into the embrace of worldly challenges that would test his spirit. In contrast, Abraham's faithfulness in the face of adversity blossomed into a rich relationship with God, who reassured him of His promises.

Ultimately, the journey of Abraham and Lot serves as a reminder of the transformative strength found in family connections and shared visions. Even as they walked divergent paths, their bond endured, reuniting in times of need—most notably when Lot faced dangers that threatened his very existence. Abraham's unwavering compassion shone through as he rallied a rescue for Lot, showcasing the beauty of familial loyalty and the courageous heart that loves beyond bounds.

Through trials and triumphs, the saga of Abraham and Lot illustrates that while journeys may diverge, the ties that bind us—nurtured by faith and shared dreams—remain ever strong. Their story inspires us to honor our family bonds, pursue our divine callings, and cherish the moments when we can come together, even amidst life's uncertainties.

UNPACKING THIS STORY GENESIS 12:5

> *"Abram took Sarai his wife and Lot his brother's son, and all their possessions that they had gathered, and the people that they had acquired in Haran, and they set out to go to the land of Canaan."*

This verse marks the beginning of a significant chapter in biblical history, where Abraham, later known as the father of many nations, begins his divinely-directed migration. It also introduces the pivotal relationship between Abraham and his nephew Lot.

This passage also highlights the importance of kinship and mutual support in ancient times. Abraham's decision to take Lot under his wing is a testament to the strength of their family bond. In a world where survival often depended on one's family and community, the support system provided by such relationships was indispensable.

The significance of this verse extends beyond its historical context. For modern readers, it underscores the value of family unity and the shared vision that can guide individuals through life's uncertainties. It serves as a reminder that the bonds we form are crucial in navigating the challenges and blessings that come our way.

THE JOURNEY OF ABRAHAM AND LOT

The geographical and cultural journeys undertaken by Abraham and Lot are significant aspects of their story. Leaving Haran and traveling to Canaan was not merely a physical move but a leap of faith driven by a divine promise. This migration marked the beginning of a new chapter in their lives and the future of humanity. It was a journey filled with both opportunities and challenges.

The separation of Abraham and Lot in Genesis 13 is a pivotal moment in their story. Due to disputes over grazing land, they amicably decided to part ways, with Lot choosing the fertile plains of Jordan and Abraham settling in the land of Canaan. This decision, although driven by practical needs, also symbolized their individual paths and personal growth.

The places they visited and settled in held cultural and spiritual significance. Canaan, the land promised to Abraham and his descendants, represented a new beginning and a fulfillment of God's covenant. Lot's choice of the plains of Jordan, near the cities of Sodom and Gomorrah, would later lead to further trials and tribulations, showcasing the far-reaching consequences of our decisions.

Through their journeys, Abraham and Lot demonstrated resilience, adaptability, and faith. Their willingness to venture into the unknown and face the challenges that came their way serves as an inspiration for modern readers, reminding us of the importance of trust and vision in our own life's journeys.

FAMILY DYNAMICS AND SHARED VISIONS

The relationship between Abraham and Lot is a testament to the power of family dynamics and shared visions. Despite their different paths, their bond endured, strengthened by mutual love and respect. They supported each other in times of need, showcasing the beauty of familial loyalty.

Their shared vision of prosperity, guided by faith in God's promises, fueled their resolve and sustained them through challenging times. It also served as a reminder that our individual journeys are intertwined with those we hold dear. As they say, "a rising tide lifts all boats." The success and blessings received by one can positively impact others, highlighting the importance of collaboration and support within families.

Nurturing Family Bonds in Today's World

In the spirit of the strategic partnership between Abraham and Lot, we are reminded of the profound value inherent in family bonds. These connections form the cornerstone of our support systems, providing us with strength, compassion, and resilience in times of need. To nurture, grow, and protect these vital relationships today, we must first cultivate open communication, allowing for honest dialogue that fosters understanding and empathy. By sharing our dreams and challenges, we create a safe space where love can flourish.

Engaging in shared experiences—whether through

family gatherings, traditions, or simply spending quality time together—adds layers of richness to our bonds. It is through these moments that we create lasting memories and a sense of belonging. Additionally, we can protect our family connections by modeling unconditional love and forgiveness, embracing imperfections, and navigating conflicts with grace. In doing so, we mirror the unwavering support exemplified by Abraham in his relationship with Lot, reinforcing the idea that, even when paths diverge, the ties that bind us remain unbreakable, nourished by faith, compassion, and shared vision. As we honor these sacred relationships, we can ensure that they flourish, resilient and vibrant, amidst the challenges and blessings of life.

The Power of Faith and Shared Visions

In the spirit of the strategic partnership between Abraham and Lot, faith emerges as a guiding light that transforms our individual and collective journeys. It is through unwavering belief in a higher purpose that we find the courage to step into the unknown, much like Abraham did when he left Haran for the promise of Canaan. Faith empowers us to rise above our fears and challenges, allowing us to navigate the winding roads of life with confidence and grace. When we anchor ourselves in faith, we align our hearts and minds with a vision that transcends our personal desires and connects us to a shared mission—be it within our families or communities.

Shared visions are equally powerful, weaving together

the dreams and aspirations of those we hold dear. They create a tapestry of unity, reminding us that while our paths may diverge, we are ultimately working toward common goals. The bond between Abraham and Lot exemplifies this beautifully; despite their different choices, the essence of their partnership lay in their shared vision of prosperity, guided by faith in God's promises. This collaborative spirit invites us to celebrate our unique contributions while recognizing that together we can achieve greatness. As we nurture our family bonds through open dialogue and mutual understanding, we cultivate an environment where faith and shared visions flourish, inspiring transformative growth within ourselves and our loved ones. Let us embrace this divine connection, allowing it to illuminate our paths and empower our journeys.

Embracing Life's Uncertainties with Courage

In the spirit of the strategic partnership between Abraham and Lot, the journey of life is often fraught with uncertainties that beckon us to embrace them with courage. Much like Abraham, who stepped into the unknown with faith guiding his every move, we too must cultivate the bravery to confront our own unknowns. These moments of uncertainty can be daunting, yet they also serve as gateways to profound growth and transformation. When we muster the strength to lean into life's unpredictability, we discover hidden resilience within ourselves and open our hearts to new possibilities.

Embracing uncertainty invites a deeper connection with our inner wisdom and intuition. It fosters a spirit of exploration, urging us to redefine our comfort zones and venture beyond them. Just as Lot faced the challenges posed by his choice to dwell near Sodom and Gomorrah, we may find ourselves navigating complexities that call for discernment and adaptability. In these instances, it is essential to remember that each challenge is not merely an obstacle but a stepping stone towards our ultimate purpose.

Let us embody the courage to view uncertainties as opportunities for growth, allowing our faith and shared visions to illuminate our paths. By embracing the unknown collectively—much like Abraham and Lot did—we foster unity and support, reminding ourselves that we are never alone in our journeys. Together, let us stand as pillars of strength and encouragement, inspiring one another to embrace whatever lies ahead with open hearts and steadfast spirits, knowing that through challenges, we are continually becoming our truest selves.

A LEGACY OF LOVE AND FAITH

As we conclude this chapter on Abraham and Lot, we reflect on their enduring legacy of love, faith, and shared visions that transcended generations. Their journey illustrates a sacred bond grounded in compassion and understanding, showcasing how familial ties can offer strength and resilience amid life's challenges. By nurturing our own family connections, we cultivate unwavering support that fortifies our bonds, ensuring they remain unbreakable even in the face of uncertainty.

In embracing the power of faith, we align ourselves with a higher purpose, allowing it to guide our actions and decisions as we navigate the winding paths before us. Let us honor the timeless lessons learned from Abraham and Lot, fostering a spirit of unity and collaboration that inspires not only our families but also our communities. Together, with hearts anchored in love and visions shared, we can create a future that reflects our deepest aspirations, uplifting one another as we journey toward the promise of a brighter tomorrow.

MOSES AND AARON

UNITED FOR A DIVINE CALLING

Exodus 4:14-16

In the heart of Egypt, amidst the gentle whispers of the desert winds and the poignant cries of an oppressed people, two brothers stood on the precipice of destiny. Moses, a former prince of Egypt, turned shepherd, was called by God to be Israel's deliverer. Born into a Jewish family and rescued from the Nile as a baby, God had already drafted a monumental chapter in the scrolls of time, one that would intertwine his fate with that of his brother, Aaron.

In a secluded corner of the wilderness, where the sun kissed the earth with its golden rays and the air shimmered with the unheralded tones of destiny, Moses encountered a sight that would forever alter the course of his life and ultimately history—a burning bush that was ablaze but not being consumed. The radiant glow of this miraculous event beckoned him closer and it was here that the voice of God erupted from the flames. The sacred commission to lead God's children out of the land of bondage to the promised land echoed through the canyon of his heart.

In that sacred moment at the burning bush, God revealed profound truths through extraordinary signs. The rod, once a mere tool of a shepherd, transformed into a serpent, embodying the fear and chaos that often reign in human hearts. Yet, as Moses grasped it once more, it returned to his hand, restored to a rod, signifying that God holds dominion over nature and the ability to convert our fears into instruments of divine purpose.

Then, with a gentle yet powerful command, Moses was instructed to thrust his hand into his bosom, and when he withdrew it, it was leprous, a stark reminder of human frailty and sin. Yet, in an act of divine grace, he thrust it in again, and it emerged whole, cleansed and renewed. This miraculous transformation speaks to the essence of God's calling—the ability to turn our brokenness into wholeness, illustrating that through faith and obedience, even the most flawed can be used for remarkable purposes.

These miracles were not merely demonstrations of power; they were affirmations of God's unwavering support for Moses and Aaron, marking the profound connection that would lead the Israelites out of bondage. In that sacred exchange, God inspired a partnership rooted in trust, reminding us all that He equips us with the strength to navigate our own journeys of transformation.

However, even in the face of such a divine mandate, Moses felt the weight of his own weakness and insecurities. He hesitated, his voice trembling like a leaf in the wind, burdened by the stutter that had trailed him through his life. "How can I speak to Pharaoh? Who am I, a humble shepherd, to approach the might of Egypt?" Yet, in the midst of his doubt, God's compassion shone forth like a beacon of light, assuring him of his worth and strength. "Fear not," the Lord declared, "for your brother Aaron shall be your voice." God's master plan had been revealed. Aaron, his elder brother, a voice of affirmation and courage would accompany him on this task.

With a heart aflame with purpose, Moses embraced this unexpected partnership. Together, they were like the sun and the moon, complementing each other's strengths and illuminating the path ahead. Aaron, a man endowed with the gift of oratory, became the voice that resonated in the courts of Egypt. Where Moses faltered, Aaron soared, articulating the very words that would demand freedom for their people. Their union was not merely of flesh and blood; it was a sacred commission orchestrated by God Himself, a tapestry woven with a purpose so profound that it would echo through generations.

As they stood before Pharaoh, the air thick with tension and uncertainty, a deep transformation began to unfold. The powerful words spoken by Aaron, inspired by the heavenly directives imparted to Moses, rang with fierce conviction, demanding liberation from oppression. God said,

"Let my people go!"

With each declaration, the hearts of the Israelites began to stir, rekindling their faith in a promise once thought lost to time.

THE HOLY PARTNERSHIP IN THE WILDERNESS

After ten long plagues and immense suffering upon the Egyptian people, Pharaoh finally released the children of Israel into their destiny. As they began to embark upon their journey of liberation, Moses and Aaron, along with approximately three million Israelites ventured into the wilderness journey. In this sacred expanse, Moses emerged as the steadfast leader, guiding the Israelites through trials and tribulations with unwavering faith. He became a beacon of hope, for it was through his intimate dialogues with God that divine wisdom flowed, illuminating the path ahead. Moses bore the weight of a nation on his shoulders, directing their steps while nurturing their spirits, always reminding them of their covenant with Jehovah.

In contrast, Aaron stood as the High Priest, a role that transcended mere titles; it was a sacred calling. Clad in beautiful priestly garments, Aaron embodied the bridge between the people and God, offering sacrifices and prayers as sweet incense ascended to the heavens. His compassionate heart resonated with the struggles and joys of the people, as he interceded on their behalf.

Together, Moses and Aaron personified a divine partnership; one fostering leadership forged in the fires of experience, and the other nurturing the spiritual essence of the community. Their bond exemplified the undeniable truth that, within the realm of faith, believers are called to support one another, drawing strength from both their differences and their unity. In the wilderness, they discovered that their holy partnership was not just a means to an end, but a testament to the sacred journey they shared, with God at the center, guiding them toward a promised future. This was more than a mere alliance; it was the strategic partnership ordained by Heaven for the deliverance of an entire nation.

Thus, Moses and Aaron ventured forth, bound not just by blood but by an extraordinary purpose—an unwavering commitment to serve JHVH God and the people of Israel.

THE EVERLASTING BOND BETWEEN MOSES AND AARON

In the grand tapestry of religious history, few relationships stand out as profoundly as that of Moses and Aaron. Their story is not just a tale of two brothers but a testament to the power of unity, faith, and shared purpose. For the serious Bible student, the saga of Moses and Aaron offers rich insights into leadership, divine calling, and the enduring impact of their partnership.

The story of Moses and Aaron begins with their early lives, shedding light on their upbringing and the divine paths they were destined to walk. Moses, born in Egypt under the shadow of Pharaoh's oppressive decree, was miraculously saved by Pharaoh's daughter and raised in the royal palace. Aaron, his elder brother, remained with their Hebrew family, growing up among the enslaved Israelites.

While Moses enjoyed the privileges of Egyptian royalty, Aaron experienced the harsh realities of oppression. This divergence in their early experiences would later enrich their understanding and approach to leadership. Moses, with his princely education, and Aaron, with his deep connection to the people, brought complementary strengths to their divine mission.

The pivotal moment in their lives came when God called Moses from the burning bush, instructing him to lead the Israelites out of Egypt. Moses, hesitant and aware of his own limitations, was reassured by God's provision of Aaron as his spokesperson.

> *"He will speak to the people for you, and it will be as if he were your mouth and as if you were God to him"* - Exodus 4:16.

This divine arrangement highlighted the importance of their partnership in fulfilling God's call.

Aaron's role was not merely supportive; it was integral to their mission. His eloquence and familiarity with the Hebrew people complemented Moses' prophetic vision and leadership. United, they confronted Pharaoh, performed miracles, and miraculously guided the Israelites past the Red Sea and through the wilderness, each fulfilling their role in God's magnificent plan.

Moses and Aaron's leadership styles were as distinct as their backgrounds. Moses, often seen as the lawgiver and mediator between God and the people, embodied a visionary and sometimes solitary leadership. Aaron, on the other hand, excelled in his role as a high priest, a mediator of rituals, and a leader who connected deeply with the people.

Their leadership, however, was not without challenges. They faced rebellions, doubts, and the immense burden of guiding a nation through unchartered lands. Yet, their unwavering faith and reliance on God and each other, strengthened their resolve. Moses' patience and Aaron's empathy created a balanced leadership that sustained the Israelites through their trials.

LESSONS FOR TODAY

The story of Moses and Aaron is not confined to ancient scriptures; it resonates with contemporary themes of leadership, faith, and community. Their partnership teaches us the value of collaboration and mutual support in achieving great endeavors. Just as Moses and Aaron complemented each other, modern leaders can benefit from recognizing and leveraging the diverse strengths within their teams.

In the spirit of Moses and Aaron's remarkable journey, we can draw inspiration for nurturing sacred partnerships in our own lives. Here are some ways to foster connections that embody unity, faith, and shared purpose:

- **Open Communication**

Create safe spaces for dialogue where perspectives can be shared freely. By encouraging open communication, partners build trust and understanding, allowing for deeper connection and cooperation. This exchange of thoughts fosters empathy and aligns intentions, much like the dialogues Moses had with God and Aaron.

- **Recognize Complementary Strengths**

Each individual brings unique strengths to a partnership. Embrace these differences and view them as assets rather than obstacles. Just as Moses' leadership and Aaron's compassion mattered to their mission, recognizing and valuing the unique contributions of each person can empower collaborative efforts that achieve collective goals.

- **Shared Vision and Goals**

Establish a common purpose that resonates at the core of the partnership. By aligning on shared values and collective aims, partners create a sense of belonging and direction. Much like Moses and Aaron strived towards the liberation of their people, a shared vision can inspire teams to work together harmoniously towards a brighter future.

- **Support Through Challenges**

Encourage one another during difficult times. Just as Moses and Aaron faced trials and tribulations together, providing emotional and spiritual support can strengthen resilience and foster a sense of unity. This bond becomes a refuge amidst adversity, reminding partners that they are not alone on their journey.

- **Celebrate Achievements Together**

Take time to acknowledge and celebrate milestones, both big and small. Recognizing achievements reinforces the strength of the partnership and cultivates gratitude, reminding everyone involved of the progress made. This celebration embodies the spirit of gratitude, illuminating the path of the journey ahead.

By embracing these principles, individuals can cultivate sacred partnerships that reflect the divine connection exemplified by Moses and Aaron, empowering communities to thrive in faith, love, and unity.

Their unwavering faith amidst adversity provides a powerful example for believer's today. In times of doubt or challenge, the steadfastness of Moses and Aaron reminds us to trust in a higher purpose and remain committed to our callings. Their story also highlights the significance of community and compassion, urging us to foster connections and support one another in our journeys.

* * *

THE EPIC true story of Moses and Aaron is a timeless beacon of unity, faith, and divine calling. Their partnership exemplifies how shared leadership and complementary strengths can achieve extraordinary outcomes.

As we reflect on their legacy, we are reminded of the enduring impact of faith-driven leadership and community. Whether leading a congregation, a team, or simply navigating personal challenges, the principles embodied by Moses and Aaron can guide us toward greater fulfillment and purpose.

In closing, remember that the power of shared leadership and faith is as relevant today as it was in ancient times. May the story of Moses and Aaron continue to uplift and guide us in our own divine callings.

RUTH AND NAOMI

THE POWER OF COMMITMENT

In the ancient land of Moab, two young women, Ruth and Orpah, stood at a crossroads of destiny, cloaked in the shadows of loss and sorrow. Their hearts were heavy, mourning the passing of their beloved husbands, yet their spirits fluttered with the delicate whispers of hope. Naomi, their mother-in-law, an emblem of resilience wrapped in weary grace, prepared to return to Bethlehem. She carried the promise of her people—a land flowing with milk and honey, a sacred home steeped in the echoes of faith.

As Naomi spoke, her voice wove tales of a God who blessed the faithful and brought forth life from barrenness. The choice lay before them like a radiant horizon at dawn. Orpah, though filled with love for Naomi, found herself hesitating, tethered to the familiar comforts of Moab. With a heart torn, she embraced Naomi and chose the path of security, returning to her mother's house, her decision born from fear rather than faith.

But Ruth, with a heart ablaze and eyes shimmering like the stars overhead, felt an unwavering pull towards the unknown. "Where you go, I will go; where you stay, I will stay," she declared, her voice a melody of determination. Ruth's decision was not just a promise to Naomi but a sacred pledge to walk in the footsteps of the Almighty. Unbeknown to her, she chose the path that would lead her to the blessing of Abraham—a destiny ripened with potential and Divine favor.

Together, Ruth and Naomi journeyed towards Bethlehem, their bond fortified by shared purpose. As they entered the city, the shadows of doubt and despair began to lift, revealing a future bright with possibility. Ruth's unwavering commitment bore fruit when she gleaned in the fields of Boaz, a kinsman of Naomi. There, amidst the golden grains kissed by sunlight, Ruth's beauty and strength captivated Boaz, igniting a connection that transcended the barriers of status and lineage.

Ruth's choice, rooted in love and dedication, led her not only to a life of abundance but to the fulfillment of God's promise. Through Ruth and Boaz, a lineage formed —one that would ultimately bear the name of David, leading to the extraordinary journey of salvation. Orpah's path may have seemed safe, yet it diverged into the fading echoes of history, while Ruth's daring leap of faith turned into a legacy of hope, courage, and divine blessing.

In the shimmering tapestry of their lives, we are reminded that even at the crossroad of choices, it is the faith to embrace the unknown that ushers in abundant blessings. Ruth's story inspires us to follow our hearts, to lean into the spirit of commitment, and to trust the sacred journey that unfolds when we choose love over fear.

THE CONCEPT OF COMMITMENT

Commitment is the glue that binds relationships, communities, and even civilizations. It represents a solemn promise to remain steadfast, regardless of the circumstances. This principle transcends all aspects of life—personal, professional, and spiritual.

In personal relationships, commitment is about loyalty and support through both joyful and challenging times. The Bible offers numerous examples of such dedication. One poignant instance is the relationship between David and Jonathan. In 1 Samuel 18:3, it is written,

> *"Then Jonathan made a covenant with David because he loved him as his own soul."*

Their bond was characterized by unwavering support and mutual respect, even in the face of adversity.

Professionally, commitment involves dedication to one's job, responsibilities, and colleagues. Colossians 3:23 encourages this ethos:

> *"Whatever you do, work heartily, as for the Lord and not for men."*

This scripture emphasizes that our dedication in the workplace is not just a duty to our employers but a service to God Himself. It reminds us to bring our best selves to our work, fostering an environment of integrity and excellence.

Spiritually, commitment is about fostering an unyielding faith and trust in a higher power. The story of Abraham is a profound example of this. In Genesis 22:2-3, God commands Abraham to sacrifice his son Isaac, and despite the unimaginable nature of this request, Abraham's faith does not waver. His readiness to commit to God's will, even at great personal cost, showcases the depth of spiritual dedication.

Commitment is not just a word; it is an action backed by intent and perseverance. When we commit, we declare that we are willing to invest our time, energy, and resources into something larger than ourselves. Philippians 3:13-14 encapsulates this spirit:

> *"Brothers and sisters, I do not consider myself yet to have taken hold of it. But one thing I do: Forgetting what is behind and straining toward what is ahead, I press on toward the goal to win the prize for which God has called me heavenward in Christ Jesus."*

Understanding the depth and breadth of commitment is crucial. It requires us to transcend our individual desires and align with greater purposes—be it in our personal lives, our professional endeavors, or our spiritual journeys. Commitment, when practiced with sincerity and reverence, fosters a sense of connection and Divine protection, revealing the profound truths of our existence and guiding us towards a more fulfilled and purposeful life.

BUILDING STRONG RELATIONSHIPS

The story of Ruth and Naomi stands as a timeless testament to the power of commitment in building strong, enduring relationships. Their bond, deeply rooted in loyalty, mutual respect, and unwavering support, offers profound lessons on how we can cultivate and sustain meaningful connections in our own lives.

In the Book of Ruth, we see Ruth's extraordinary commitment to her mother-in-law Naomi, even after the death of her husband. Ruth 1:16-17 captures this beautifully:

> *"But Ruth replied, 'Don't urge me to leave you or to turn back from you. Where you go I will go, and where you stay I will stay. Your people will be my people and your God my God. Where you die I will die, and there I will be buried. May the Lord deal with me, be it ever so severely, if even death separates you and me."*

This declaration of loyalty is a powerful example of the depth and strength that commitment can bring to a relationship.

In our personal lives, the commitment exemplified by Ruth and Naomi can be mirrored in our friendships. True friends stand by each other through thick and thin, offering support and understanding in both joyful and challenging times. Proverbs 17:17 reminds us,

> "A friend loves at all times, and a brother is born for a time of adversity."

This scripture underscores that genuine friendships thrive on a foundation of mutual respect and unwavering support, much like Ruth and Naomi's relationship.

Commitment is equally essential in marriages, serving as the bedrock upon which love and trust are built. Couples who are dedicated to each other navigate life's storms together, growing stronger with each challenge they face. Ephesians 5:25-28 provides insight into this sacred bond:

> "Husbands, love your wives, just as Christ loved the church and gave himself up for her to make her holy... In this same way, husbands ought to love their wives as their own bodies. He who loves his wife loves himself."

Here, the call for selfless love and commitment in marriage mirrors the unwavering dedication seen in Ruth and Naomi's story.

Commitment in relationships is about showing up, being present, and standing by each other through life's ups and downs. It involves a conscious decision to invest time, energy, and emotional resources into another person. Ecclesiastes 4:9-10 speaks to this principle:

"Two are better than one because they have a good return for their labor."

This verse highlights the power of partnership and how commitment to one another can bring about a fruitful and fulfilling life. In all our relationships, let us strive for a deep sense of commitment, mirroring the loyalty, mutual respect, and unwavering support exemplified by Ruth and Naomi. As we do so, we will create strong foundations that will withstand the tests of time and lead us towards deeper connections with those around us. So let us embrace commitment in all aspects of our lives, for it is an essential element in building strong relationships that last a lifetime.

PRACTICAL APPLICATIONS

In practical terms, applying the lessons from Ruth and Naomi's story means cultivating relationships marked by:

- **Loyalty** - standing by each other through thick and thin, even in the face of difficult circumstances.

- **Mutual respect** - acknowledging and valuing the unique qualities and contributions of each person in the relationship.

- **Unwavering support** - being present and

offering encouragement, help, and understanding when needed.

- **Selflessness** - prioritizing the well-being and needs of others above our own desires.

- **Intentionality** - making a conscious effort to invest time, energy, and emotional resources into building strong relationships.

By embodying these principles in our relationships, we can experience deeper connections, mutual growth, and lasting bonds.

Building strong relationships requires more than just affection; it demands a steadfast commitment like to that of Ruth and Naomi.

"But let your communication be, Yea, yea; Nay, nay: for whatsoever is more than these cometh of evil" - Matthew 5:37.

Let love be the driving force. For when we commit to love and honor others as God has called us to do, we open ourselves up to a greater understanding of our purpose and a more fulfilling life journey. Embrace commitment wholeheartedly, for it is truly the foundation of strong relationships that can withstand the tests of time.

EMBRACING COMMITMENT IN EVERY ASPECT OF LIFE

Commitment is the cornerstone of meaningful connections and transformative progress. In our communities, workplaces, schools, hospitals, and educational facilities, the act of committing ourselves to a cause greater than our own can spark profound change and inspire others to follow suit.

In our neighborhoods and towns, commitment fosters trust and unity. By dedicating time to local initiatives, participating in community events, and offering support to neighbors, we weave a fabric of interconnectedness that strengthens the entire community. When we commit to one another, we create a sanctuary of mutual trust and collective resilience.

In professional environments, commitment is the driving force behind excellence and innovation. It is through our unwavering dedication to our roles, our colleagues, and our organizational missions that we achieve true success. By committing to continuous improvement, ethical practices, and collaborative efforts, we elevate not only our work but also the spirits of those around us, creating a workplace that thrives on shared purpose and visionary goals.

Educational institutions serve as the bedrock for future generations. When educators, students, and parents collectively commit to the pursuit of knowledge, personal growth, and community service, they establish a vibrant learning environment. This commitment instills values of perseverance, empathy, and leadership in young minds, empowering them to become the compassionate and capable leaders of tomorrow.

Commitment in educational facilities transcends the confines of traditional teaching. It encompasses a dedication to lifelong learning, personal development, and societal contribution. Educators who commit to innovative teaching methods and inclusive practices inspire their students to explore the depths of their potential. This dedication ensures that education becomes a transformative journey, enriching lives and fostering a deep connection to the world.

In healthcare settings, commitment is synonymous with compassion and care. Medical professionals who commit to their patients' well-being go beyond mere treatment; they offer hope, comfort, and reassurance. By embracing a holistic approach to healing, where each patient is treated with dignity and respect, healthcare providers foster an atmosphere of trust and divine protection, aiding in the recovery process both physically and spiritually.

In essence, embracing commitment in every facet of life enriches our experiences and strengthens our bonds. As we step forward with genuine dedication, we not only uplift ourselves but also create ripples of profound impact that reverberate through our communities and beyond. Let us commit, with sincere hearts and open minds, to the paths that lead us toward a brighter, more connected future.

OVERCOMING CHALLENGES WITH COMMITMENT

One of the most profound lessons from Ruth and Naomi's story is the role of commitment in overcoming challenges. Ruth and Naomi faced numerous hardships—bereavement, poverty, and uncertainty about the future. Yet, their unwavering commitment to each other and to their faith provided the strength they needed to persevere. In our own lives, commitment can be a guiding light in times of adversity. When faced with obstacles, a committed mindset helps us stay focused and resilient. It reminds us that challenges are temporary, but the rewards of staying true to our commitments are everlasting.

Actions to Overcome Challenges with Commitment

1. **Find Strength in Faith:** Just as Ruth and Naomi drew strength from their faith, we too can find solace and resilience by committing to our lives to God. Regular prayer, meditation, or attending faith-based gatherings can anchor us during turbulent times.
2. **Support Each Other:** Emulate Ruth's dedication to Naomi by building a network of support. Commit to being there for your loved ones, offering a helping hand and a listening ear whenever needed. Together, we can face and overcome any challenge.

3. **Stay Focused on Your Goals:** When adversity strikes, it's easy to lose sight of our long-term goals. A steadfast commitment to our aspirations can help keep us on track. Write down your goals and regularly revisit them to maintain clarity and motivation.
4. **Embrace Positivity:** A committed mindset isn't just about persistence; it's also about maintaining a positive outlook. Surround yourself with uplifting influences—be it people, literature, or activities—that reinforce your commitment to overcoming challenges.
5. **Celebrate Small Wins:** Recognize and celebrate the small victories along your journey. These moments of success, no matter how minor, serve as reminders of your progress and fuel your commitment to continue pushing forward.

Commitment is also a pathway to personal and spiritual growth. Ruth's commitment to Naomi and her new faith led to remarkable blessings. Ruth eventually marries Boaz, a man of great wealth and integrity, and becomes an ancestor of King David and, ultimately, Jesus Christ. This divine blessing was a direct result of Ruth's unwavering commitment. In our spiritual journeys, commitment to our faith helps us grow closer to God. It deepens our understanding, strengthens our resolve, and opens the door to divine blessings.

Actions to Achieve Personal and Spiritual Growth

1. **Dedicate Time for Reflection:** Allocate regular time for self-reflection and spiritual contemplation. Journaling, meditating, or simply spending quiet moments in nature can enhance your spiritual understanding and personal insight.
2. **Engage in Faith-Based Activities:** Participate actively in your faith community. Whether through volunteering, attending services, or joining study groups, these activities can deepen your connection with your faith and foster spiritual growth.
3. **Seek Mentors and Guides:** Find mentors or spiritual guides who inspire you and can offer wisdom and guidance on your journey. Their experiences and insights can illuminate your path and strengthen your commitment.
4. **Practice Gratitude:** Cultivate a habit of gratitude by regularly acknowledging the blessings in your life. This practice not only uplifts your spirit but also fortifies your commitment to your faith and personal growth.
5. **Act with Integrity:** Stay true to your values and principles, even when it's challenging. Acting with integrity reinforces your commitment and builds a foundation of trust and respect, both for yourself and others.

By embracing these actions, we can navigate life's challenges with grace and achieve profound personal and spiritual growth. Just as Ruth and Naomi's story teaches us, unwavering commitment leads to enduring rewards and divine blessings. Let us commit to our faith and each other, knowing that every step taken with a sincere heart paves the way for a brighter, more connected future.

REFLECTING ON OUR OWN COMMITMENTS

The story of Ruth and Naomi invites us to reflect deeply on our own commitments and the strength of our relationships. Are we as devoted to our loved ones, communities, and faith as Ruth was to Naomi? Ruth's unwavering loyalty and support through hardship serves as a powerful example for us all. When challenges arise, do we stand firm by our commitments, or do we waver in the face of adversity?

Take a moment to consider the areas in your life where you can strengthen your commitment. Whether it's being more present in your relationships by actively listening and engaging with others, dedicating more time to community service to make a meaningful impact in the lives of those around you, or deepening your spiritual practices through regular reflection and connection, there are always opportunities to grow. Embracing these commitments not only enriches our own lives but also fosters stronger bonds within our families, communities, and faith. Let's strive to embody the same dedication that Ruth demonstrated, nurturing our connections and serving as a source of support and inspiration for others.

Lastly, let's not keep these valuable insights to

ourselves. It's important to share what you've learned about the transformative power of commitment with your community. Encourage others to delve into the inspiring story of Ruth and Naomi, highlighting their unwavering loyalty and the profound lessons it offers about relationships and perseverance. Engage in thoughtful discussions about the importance of commitment across various spheres of life—personal, professional, and spiritual. By actively sharing our insights and experiences, we can inspire others to cultivate a spirit of unwavering commitment in their own lives, fostering a supportive environment where commitment and dedication are valued and prioritized. Together, we can create a ripple effect that amplifies the impact of these essential values in our communities.

In conclusion, the story of Ruth and Naomi serves as a profound testament to the transformative power of commitment and loyalty. Their unwavering love and steadfast support for one another, even in the face of immense hardship and societal challenges, demonstrate the depth of their bond and faith. Ruth's bold decision to leave her homeland and follow Naomi was not just an act of loyalty; it was a courageous step towards a new life that ultimately led to divine blessings, including Ruth's place in the lineage of King David and, ultimately, Jesus Christ. This legacy continues to inspire us today, reminding us of the importance of commitment in our own lives.

By understanding and applying the principles of commitment—such as loyalty, sacrifice, and faithfulness—we can build stronger relationships with our family, friends, and communities. These principles encourage us to invest time and effort into nurturing our connections, fostering environments where people can thrive and grow together. As we navigate our own journeys, it's essential to take a moment to reflect on the commitments we've made, whether in our personal or professional lives. Consider how you can deepen these commitments, perhaps by being more present, supportive, or open to change.

Moreover, sharing these insights with your community can create a ripple effect, inspiring others to evaluate their own commitments and challenges. Together, by fostering a culture of unwavering commitment, we can create a world filled with extraordinary blessings, mutual support, and lasting impact. Let us encourage one another to embrace the power of commitment and witness the positive transformations it can bring to our lives and the lives of those around us.

DAVID AND JONATHAN

A BOND OF LOYALTY

As the sun began to set over the rolling hills of Israel, painting the horizon with strokes of gold and crimson, two young men stood poised at the edge of destiny—David, the shepherd with the heart of a lion, and Jonathan, the noble son of King Saul, embodying the elegance of a warrior. Their worlds, though forged by differing destinies, converged in a powerful alliance that would echo through the ages. It was a time when the air was thick with anticipation, voices of men stirring with ambition, and the fragrance of promise hung like a veil over the land.

In the midst of uncertainty and strife, as shadows of hostility stretched across the kingdom, David and Jonathan discovered an unshakeable bond woven together by faith, trust, and mutual respect. From the very first time their eyes met—Jonathan, cloaked in the royal garb of his lineage, and David, adorned in the humble clothing of a shepherd—their hearts recognized something profound. David, freshly anointed, bore the weight of a divine call, while Jonathan stood at a crossroads, caught between loyalty to his father and the allure of a friendship that would redirect the course of history.

Together, they shared spirited conversations under the ancient olive trees that whispered secrets of yesteryears. As the breeze danced through the leaves, the young men spoke of dreams that dared to defy the status quo—dreams of a kingdom united under love rather than fear, of a people led by benevolence rather than tyranny. With laughter bubbling like a brook and deep conversation flowing like the River Jordan, they forged a strategy that balanced courage and wisdom, loyalty and vision. Jonathan, a faithful friend, displayed the remarkable ability to look beyond the crown he could inherit, seeing instead a future where David would wear the mantle of leadership guided by righteousness.

In their clandestine meetings, each plotted and schemed with a purpose as vibrant as the colors of the sunset that enveloped them. Jonathan, who had everything to lose, stood resolute in his belief that true power lay in serving a higher calling. He offered David more than shield and sword; he offered him alliance, a brotherhood that transcended familial ties and earthly power. This was a partnership rooted in mutual sacrifice and the courage to stand strong in the face of adversity.

The Warning

As the storm clouds of conflict gathered ominously over the kingdom, Jonathan awakened to the weight of his inheritance—not merely the crown that destined him for kingship, but the pressing responsibility to protect his beloved friend, David. The bond they forged was a sanctuary during turbulent times, and now, it faced its greatest test. In an act of unwavering loyalty, Jonathan devised a plan to warn David of the impending danger posed by King Saul's wrath.

Under the gentle embrace of the morning sun, they agreed to meet in the fields. Jonathan armed himself with bow and arrow, symbols of strength and precision, but today they would carry a message of compassion and urgency. With great care, Jonathan shot arrows far beyond their meeting place, a signal for David that would communicate the intentions of King Saul and change the course of their lives.

As the arrows soared into the vast sky, they served as both a warning and a promise.

> *"If I say to the boy, 'Look, the arrows are on this side of you; take them,' then come, for it is safe for you,"*

Jonathan proclaimed softly, his voice laced with the trembling of a faithful heart.

> *"But if I say, 'Look, the arrows are beyond you,' then go, for the Lord has sent you away."*

In that moment, their friendship transcended beyond

mere words; it was a language of the spirit, filled with the weight of loyalty and sacrifice.

David, hidden among the bushes, felt the stirrings of fear and hope intermingling within him. As he heard Jonathan's delicate messages carried on the breeze, his heart ached with both gratitude and sorrow. The knowledge that his friend was willing to expose himself to danger ignited a flame of courage within him. They understood the depths of their friendship bond; they understood that destiny often calls for profound sacrifice. In that simple gesture of a bow and arrow, Jonathan embodied the essence of true friendship—one that defies the very nature of this world to embrace the divine purpose of protecting and uplifting one another even against the fiercest of adversities.

Thus, the story of Jonathan and David unfurled like the petals of a blossoming flower, vibrant and alive, breathing life into a narrative that would inspire countless souls yearning for connection, purpose, and the courage to stand in solidarity. Through their alliance, they emerged not just as friends but as champions of a transformative hope, lighting a path towards a brighter, more compassionate future for a nation long embroiled in turmoil.

THE BENEFITS AND CHALLENGES OF A SPIRITUAL ALLIANCE

The bond between David and Jonathan extends beyond mere friendship; it exists as an emblem of spiritual partnership that nurtures growth and resilience in the face of adversity. The profound benefits of such an alliance echo through time, illuminating paths for those who seek unity in their endeavors. One of the most poignant benefits of their relationship is found in the Scriptures, where Proverbs 27:17 reminds us,

"Iron sharpens iron, and one man sharpens another."

This maxim reflects the transformative power of partnership, fostering a sanctuary of encouragement, wisdom, and strength. David, buoyed by Jonathan's unwavering loyalty, found the courage to embrace his divine calling. In our current context, harnessing the power of collaboration enables us to elevate collective strengths, overcome personal limitations, and face challenges with renewed vigor.

However, the mantle of such a partnership is not without its trials. The delicate balance between individual ambitions and shared purpose can lead to friction. As we mirror the journey of David and Jonathan, we must remain vigilant against the specters of jealousy, fear, and misunderstanding that can arise. Jonathan faced the challenge of supporting David while being loyal to his father, King Saul, a tension reminiscent of many modern-day dilemmas where allegiances may seem to clash. The biblical narrative teaches us the importance of clarity and communication, as highlighted in James 1:19,

"Let every person be quick to hear, slow to speak, slow to anger."

By fostering open dialogues and embracing vulnerability, we can navigate misunderstandings that threaten the bonds we create.

To cultivate an environment where mutual success flourishes, we must heed the biblical exhortation found in Ecclesiastes 4:9-10:

"Two are better than one, because they have a good reward for their toil. For if they fall, one will lift up his fellow."

Let us strive to be those who uplift one another, celebrating the unique gifts each person brings to the partnership. By acknowledging our differences and choosing to see them as opportunities for learning and growth, we can weave a fabric of resilience that withstands the tumult of our surroundings. Engaging in acts of service, offering our talents generously, and maintaining a steadfast commitment to one another's well-being will fortify our alliances, ultimately leading to shared victories that resonate beyond ourselves.

In the vivid tapestry of life, we too can emulate the legacy of David and Jonathan, where the interplay of unity and individuality creates a harmonious melody. By recognizing the benefits and challenges of spiritual partnerships with open hearts and steadfast minds, we can cultivate a profound sense of purpose and strength that guides us through the complexities of our journey—

together, illuminating the path toward a future aligned with love and mutual respect.

THE LESSONS OF THIS STRATEGIC PARTNERSHIP

The enduring partnership between David and Jonathan invites us to reflect deeply on the essence of loyalty, sacrifice, and mutual support. Their journey reminds us that true friendship flourishes not in the absence of challenges but precisely in the way we navigate them together. The profound insights gleaned from their relationship are timeless, resonating with anyone who seeks to foster meaningful connections in their lives. Each shared moment, each act of selflessness, serves as a testament to the power of love and understanding, urging us to rise above personal fears and embrace a collective purpose.

From their unwavering bond, we learn that our journeys are interwoven, and the strength of one can uplift many. The courage David drew from Jonathan's loyalty exemplifies how support can transform vulnerability into resilience, igniting our potential to overcome obstacles. This alliance teaches us that growth is often illuminated through shared experiences; when we come together to celebrate each other's unique gifts, we weave a rich tapestry of inspiration that extends far beyond ourselves.

Moreover, the lessons encapsulated in their story inform our daily lives, encouraging us to cultivate a culture of compassion and open dialogue. As we carry these insights forward, we are reminded that the spiritual wisdom revealed through their partnership offers guidance in moments of trial and triumph alike. We can foster unity by actively listening, by being slow to anger, and by choosing understanding over discord. As we form strategic alliances within our communities, workplaces, and relationships, we harness the power of collaboration—nurturing environments where everyone feels valued.

In a world often marked by division, the legacy of David and Jonathan serves as a beacon of hope, illuminating the path we can tread together. Their story implores us to embody the virtues of patience, forgiveness, and humility. Let us embrace the divine wisdom that arises from our interconnectedness, knowing that each relationship we nurture has the potential to guide us toward greater purpose and fulfillment. As we carry these insights into our ongoing endeavors, may we sow seeds of growth and unity, allowing the spirit of compassion to flourish in every aspect of our lives.

ELIJAH AND ELISHA

PASSING THE MANTLE

2 Kings 2:9-10

In a time when the air was thick with uncertainty and the people of Israel wandered far from their true path, the flame of prophecy flickered brightly in a land shadowed by spiritual desolation. The sun dipped low, casting golden rays that danced upon the earth as Elijah, the revered prophet of the Lord, roamed the rugged hills and valleys. His heart resonated with the rhythm of of his relationship with God as he surrendered his life, a vessel through which God's voice reached the nation.

One fateful day, as the sun began its descent, splashing hues of orange and crimson across the sky, he found himself at the edge of a humble field. Here, he encountered a young man named Elisha, ploughing the earth, his hands stained with the rich soil that nourished life. There was a spark, an indescribable presence in the air, as if the very heavens were holding their breath in anticipation of what was to unfold. Elijah, feeling the weight of destiny upon him, cast his mantle onto Elisha's shoulders. It was not merely a cloak; it was a divine calling, an invitation to a spiritual transfer, a divine mantle that bore the weight of legacy and expectation.

With eyes wide and spirit ignited, Elisha heard the words unspoken—a tacit invitation to a partnership, a bond that would weave their fates together like the threads of a masterful tapestry. As the vibrant colors of the sunset reflected the myriad paths that lay before them, Elisha knew, deep within, that he was being called to a journey far greater than himself. Leaving behind the familiar comforts of his plough and the warmth of his family, he embraced the unknown, stepping into the world of prophetic service.

Together, Elijah and Elisha became a dynamic duo, traversing the rugged landscapes, from the jagged peaks of Mount Carmel to the bustling streets of Samaria. They became instruments of hope, drawing the fragmented hearts of Israel back to JHVH with fervor and compassion. Each encounter was an opportunity for transformation; through miracles and messages, healing and hope intertwined in their every move.

The sunlit days gave way to starlit nights, where they shared visions and revelations beneath the expansive sky, reflecting upon the mysteries of existence. Here, in the sacred space of their partnership, a profound bond formed—one of mutual respect, shared faith, and unwavering love for their people and God. With every challenge they faced, a vibrant dance of courage and humility blossomed, showcasing the depth of their connection. The air was electric, infused with the spirit of possibility, as they faced storms, both literal and metaphorical, together.

As Elijah's time on earth drew to a close, and he prepared to pass the mantle of prophecy to Elisha, the atmosphere crackled with anticipation and reverence. The chariot of fire and horses of heaven descended, shimmering like stars come alive in the twilight. A sense of awakening surged within Elisha's heart, for he was no longer merely a student; he had become "the prophet" ready to carry forward the torch of Israel's destiny.

In that profound moment of transition, the spirit of their strategic partnership transcended earthly bounds, forging a legacy that would inspire generations to come. Through their story, a reminder echoes: when we truly embrace our calling and align ourselves with a shared purpose, we can illuminate the world around us with the profound beauty of collaboration and divine destiny against the backdrop of JHVH's love. The mantle of faith, enriched by every vibrant thread of their journey, beckons us all to rise, inspiring us to weave our own tales of hope and transformation.

THE BIBLICAL NARRATIVE OF ELIJAH AND ELISHA

The relationship between Elijah and Elisha is a profound example of divine purpose and human connection. Elijah, the great prophet of Israel, was nearing the end of his earthly ministry. In his wisdom, he sought to ensure that his mission would continue by preparing Elisha as his successor. This preparation culminated in the symbolic act of passing the mantle, signifying the transfer of prophetic authority and responsibility.

In 2 Kings 2:9-10, we witness a poignant moment of transition:

> *"When they had crossed, Elijah said to Elisha, 'Tell me, what can I do for you before I am taken from you?' 'Let me inherit a double portion of your spirit,' Elisha replied. 'You have asked a difficult thing,' Elijah said, 'yet if you see me when I am taken from you, it will be yours—otherwise, it will not.'"*

This dialogue sets the stage for a deeper exploration of the themes of leadership, mentorship, and the role of faith in guiding decisions and actions.

The passage in 2 Kings 2:9-10 is rich with meaning and implications. Elijah's question to Elisha is not merely a formality; it is an invitation to express his deepest desires and aspirations. By asking for a double portion of Elijah's spirit, Elisha reveals his commitment to continuing Elijah's work with even greater zeal and dedication.

Elijah's response acknowledges the gravity of Elisha's request. He recognizes that such a blessing is not his to grant but is contingent upon divine approval. This underscores the importance of divine intervention in the succession of spiritual leadership, reminding us that true authority comes from God.

The condition set by Elijah—that Elisha must witness

his ascension to receive the blessing—emphasizes the need for unwavering faith and attentiveness. It is a test of Elisha's resolve and readiness to assume the mantle of leadership.

Understanding the historical and cultural contexts of this narrative enriches our appreciation of its significance. In ancient Israel, the prophetic office was not merely a role but a divine calling. Prophets were seen as intermediaries between God and the people, tasked with delivering messages of guidance, warning, and hope.

The concept of the prophetic mantle, both literal and symbolic, held deep meaning. It represented the authority and responsibility bestowed upon the prophet by God. The act of passing the mantle was a visible and tangible sign of the transfer of this sacred duty.

LESSONS FOR CONTEMPORARY FAITH COMMUNITIES

The narrative of Elijah and Elisha offers valuable lessons for contemporary faith communities and leaders. At its core, it emphasizes the importance of mentorship and the intentional preparation of successors. Elijah's investment in Elisha's development ensured the continuity of his mission and the preservation of divine guidance for Israel.

The Importance of Mentorship

Mentorship forms the very foundation upon which the growth and transformation of individuals can flourish. It is a sacred partnership, where wisdom is shared, experiences are exchanged, and hearts are ignited with passion and purpose. Just as Elijah nurtured Elisha, guiding him with love and intention, we too can embrace the transformative power of mentorship in our lives and communities. At its essence, mentorship fosters an environment of trust and encouragement, empowering mentees to explore their potential and develop their unique gifts. As we cultivate these connections, we create a tapestry of support that not only uplifts individuals but also strengthens the collective spirit of our faith communities.

Ways Successful Mentorship Happens

1. **Open Communication**: Establishing a safe space for dialogue allows mentors and mentees to share thoughts, aspirations, and concerns freely, leading to deeper understanding and connection.
2. **Setting Clear Goals**: Collaboratively identifying specific objectives helps to direct efforts and provides a roadmap for personal and spiritual growth.
3. **Active Listening**: Mentors demonstrate compassion by truly listening to their mentees, validating their experiences, and guiding them with empathy.
4. **Sharing Personal Experiences**: By recounting their own journeys, mentors can provide valuable insights and lessons learned, inspiring

mentees to navigate their paths with confidence.
5. **Encouragement and Affirmation**: Recognizing and celebrating the achievements and potential of mentees fosters a sense of belonging and motivates them to pursue their goals with enthusiasm.
6. **Providing Constructive Feedback**: Gentle, honest feedback is essential for growth, as it helps mentees identify areas for improvement while also reinforcing their strengths.
7. **Modeling Values and Behaviors**: By embodying the principles of faith and service, mentors serve as living examples of the qualities they wish to instill in their mentees.
8. **Fostering Accountability**: Encouraging mentees to take responsibility for their personal development nurtures integrity and commitment to their goals.

Through these methods, mentorship can illuminate paths toward purpose and fulfillment, creating a ripple effect of inspiration that touches countless lives. Just as Elijah and Elisha transformed Israel through their partnership, we too can ignite a legacy of faith, compassion, and leadership through investing in one another.

For today's faith leaders, this story serves as a reminder to nurture and guide the next generation. Mentorship is not just about imparting knowledge but also about fostering spiritual growth and resilience. By investing in others, leaders can create a legacy that extends beyond their lifetime.

THE INTENTIONALITY OF PREPARING OUR SUCCESSORS

In the journey of faith and leadership, one truth resounds with profound clarity: there is no success without successors. Preparing the next generation is not merely a duty; it is an act of love and intentionality that shapes the very fabric of our communities. Each of us carries within us the potential to ignite hope and inspire those who will come after us. To cultivate this future, we must consciously invest in the growth of others, sharing not just our knowledge but our hearts and spirits.

The concept of "paying it forward" resonates deeply within this context. As we nurture and support those around us, we create a legacy of compassion and strength that reverberates through time. By offering our guidance, resources, and encouragement to those who seek to follow in our footsteps, we sow the seeds of resilience and integrity. Each act of kindness propels a cycle of empowerment, encouraging others to extend their hands to lift yet another. It is in this exchange of generosity that we discover the true essence of community—a sacred bond that unites us all.

The power of community cannot be overstated; it takes a village to cultivate the leaders of tomorrow. When we come together in support of one another, we create an environment ripe for growth, innovation, and transformation. Our collective wisdom and diverse experiences form a tapestry of strength that can guide our successors on their paths. In nurturing relationships and fostering collaboration, we remind each other that we are never alone in our journeys. Together, we form a network of support, a guiding light that illuminates the way forward. As we prepare those who will carry the torch after us, we ensure that our shared vision thrives, empowering future generations to rise and soar to new heights.

CYCLES OF EMPOWERMENT

The essence of our shared journey lies in the creation and nurturing of cycles of empowerment—dynamic processes that inspire, uplift, and transform both individuals and communities. These cycles begin with a deliberate intention to support others, cultivating an environment where mutual growth and understanding can thrive. To create these empowering cycles, we must first establish a foundation of trust and openness, allowing individuals to feel safe in sharing their aspirations and vulnerabilities. By actively listening and validating their experiences, we foster a sense of belonging that ignites the fire of potential within them.

Nourishing these cycles requires ongoing commitment and compassion. Regular check-ins and encouragement serve to reinforce the bonds formed in mentorship, while the sharing of resources and knowledge enhances the skills and capabilities of those we support. Celebrating the achievements of others creates a culture of gratitude, fostering motivation and enthusiasm that propels individuals to reach even greater heights. It is during these moments of recognition that we build a strong network of support, reminding one another that we are never alone in our pursuits.

Identifying the right moment to pass the torch to the next generation is a sacred and vital aspect of nurturing cycles of empowerment. This transition often emerges organically, as the mentees demonstrate a sense of confidence, readiness, and ownership of their journey. We must be attuned to their growth and development, recognizing the signs that indicate they are prepared to take on greater responsibilities. Engaging in open conversations about their aspirations and encouraging them to step into leadership roles equips them with the courage to embrace their path. In doing so, we celebrate our own contributions while honoring their potential, ensuring that the cycles of empowerment continue to flourish for generations to come.

APPLICATION TO PERSONAL GROWTH

The story of Elijah and Elisha is not only relevant to organizational leadership but also to personal and communal growth. On a personal level, it encourages individuals to seek out mentors who can provide guidance and support in their spiritual journeys. It also challenges individuals to be open to the call to mentor others, recognizing the impact they can have on someone's life.

The journey of mentorship, as exemplified by the partnership between Elijah and Elisha, is rich with profound insights that resonate deeply within our hearts and spirits. This sacred alliance teaches us that true leadership is not a solitary pursuit but a collective endeavor rooted in trust, respect, and shared purpose. The lessons learned from such strategic partnerships extend beyond the individuals involved, weaving a tapestry of growth and unity that inspires entire communities.

As we reflect on the wisdom gleaned from this relationship, we recognize the transformative power of mentorship. Each encounter and every shared experience becomes a thread that strengthens the fabric of our connections, reminding us that we are all interconnected in this spiritual journey. The guidance we receive and offer illuminates our paths, creating a ripple effect that nurtures resilience and fosters hope. It serves as a reminder that despite our individual challenges, we have the ability to uplift one another and cultivate a sanctuary where divine wisdom can thrive.

Moreover, the insights derived from this partnership encourage us to embrace our role as both mentees and mentors. They inspire us to continually seek growth, not only in our own lives but also in the lives of those around us. By actively engaging in this cycle of giving and receiving, we create a legacy that empowers the next generation to rise, to dream, and to believe in their potential. This ongoing journey fosters a sense of belonging and community where everyone feels valued and heard, allowing divine wisdom to flow freely as we navigate our collective purpose.

In essence, the lessons learned from our strategic partnerships illuminate our path, guiding us toward a future filled with inspiration, compassion, and growth. Embracing these insights fuels our commitment to nurturing one another, ensuring that together we can reach new heights and impel the world towards a greater sense of unity and divine harmony.

REFLECTION

Reflecting on the story of Elijah and Elisha invites us to consider our own experiences with succession and spiritual mentorship. How have we been shaped by the mentors in our lives? How are we preparing to pass on our knowledge and faith to others? Engaging in discussions about these questions can deepen our understanding and commitment to the principles embodied in this story.

The story of Elijah and Elisha, with its powerful example of passing the mantle, offers timeless lessons on leadership, mentorship, and faith. Through their example, we learn the importance of preparing the next generation, nurturing spiritual growth, and fostering a sense of community.

By reflecting on this true story and applying its lessons to our own lives, we can create a legacy of faith and leadership that endures. Whether you are a seasoned leader or just beginning your spiritual journey, the story of Elijah and Elisha provides valuable insights and inspiration.

Let us continue to cultivate relationships that

empower and uplift one another, passing on the mantle of knowledge, power, and faith for generations to come. With each new generation, we have the opportunity to renew our commitment to building a better world.

"Thou therefore, my son, be strong in the grace that is in Christ Jesus. And the things that thou hast heard of me among many witnesses, the same commit thou to faithful men, who shall be able to teach others also." - 2 Timothy 2:1-2

DEBORAH AND BARAK

THERE IS STRENGTH IN UNITY

*J*udges 4:4-10
In a time when the sun-drenched hills of Canaan bore witness to conflict and strife, a formidable woman named Deborah rose like the dawn, radiant and wise. She was a prophetess and the ruling judge of her people, embodying the indomitable spirit of Israel during its tumultuous days. Beneath the shade of a palm tree, she would gather the tribes, her voice both soothing and strong, resonating with the promise of hope. The air thick, yet alive with purpose, as the people looked to her for guidance amid the oppressive shadows cast by Sisera, the iron-hearted commander of Jabin's army.

Deborah, with a heart fierce yet compassionate, sensed the stirring of change. She knew that unity was the only path to liberation. Therefore, she summoned Barak, a warrior grounded in courage but somewhat shadowed by his own doubts. As they stood upon the mountaintop, overlooking the vast expanse of their land, the sky painted in twilight hues of orange and purple, Deborah spoke of a God's vision for Israel. With certainty and grace, she called upon Barak to rally the tribes of Israel, to face their oppressors with conviction.

> *"Gather your courage, Barak,"* she said, her voice like music in the gentle breeze. *"For we are not alone in this battle. The time has come to reclaim our lands and our spirits. You shall lead, and I shall walk beside you."*

Barak, initially hesitant, found solace in her unwavering faith. He realized that strength lay not just in swords and shields, but in the word of the God. Together, they led, rallying thousands to their cause, as the air stirred with their cries of courage and determination. The path ahead was daunting, yet the warmth of Deborah's leadership ignited a fire within his heart and the hearts of those who joined their cause.

As they prepared for the impending battle, the sun broke through the clouds, illuminating the landscape as if blessing their mission. With the armies assembled, Barak led his warriors onto the battlefield, while Deborah raised her head high, declaring the Word of the God over their impending victory. Through her unwavering faith each soldier was inspired to fight not just for their survival, but for a future illuminated by righteousness, justice, and freedom.

The clashing of swords and the sounds of battle echoed through the air, a symphony of defiance and deliverance. Deborah, standing at Barak's side, called upon JHVH, lifting her voice in fervent prayer. It this moment the lessons of unity, a reminder that strength does not stem from singular valor but from the harmony of hearts united for a common purpose, could be witnessed.

Together, they forged not only a victory over Sisera but also a legacy that would inspire generations to come. Their partnership exemplified that true strength emanates from collaboration, an unwavering bond that could withstand the fiercest storms. Through Deborah and Barak's journey, the tale of their strategic alliance emerged not just as a historical account, but as a luminous testament to the power of unity and the profound spirit of cooperation that resides within the human heart.

In the echo of their story, we find ourselves called to reflect on our paths, to understand that together, through compassion and shared purpose, we too can rise above adversity, painting the canvas of our lives with the vibrant colors of strength and unity.

THE LEADERSHIP OF DEBORAH

Deborah's leadership was marked by her unwavering faith and courage, which she instilled in those around her. As a prophetess, she was able to see beyond the physical realm and call upon God for guidance. Her wisdom and foresight enabled her to unite the tribes of Israel towards a common goal, leading them towards liberation.

Her approach to leadership serves as an example for all of us - to lead with conviction, compassion, and an unwavering belief in a higher purpose. In moments of doubt or uncertainty, we can look to Deborah's strength and find inspiration to persevere on our own journeys.

Deborah stands out in Scripture as one of the few female judges in Israel. Her dual role as both a judge and a prophetess underscores her exceptional capabilities and divine appointment. In a male-dominated society, her leadership was a testament to God's sovereignty and the breaking of traditional boundaries to fulfill His purposes.

Her wisdom was acknowledged by the Israelites who sought her counsel under the Palm of Deborah. Her judgments, motivated by divine insight, were respected and trusted. This highlights not only her competence but also her deep connection with God, which was crucial in her decision-making process.

Deborah's example shows that true leadership transcends gender. It is about obedience, wisdom, and a profound commitment to God's will. Her story encourages us to recognize and uplift capable leaders regardless of societal conventions.

Deborah's courage is evident in her willingness to lead Israel during a time of oppression. The Israelites faced the Canaanite army led by Sisera, a formidable foe with superior military resources, including 900 iron chariots. Despite the daunting challenge, Deborah's faith in God's promise did not waver.

Her loyalty to God was the foundation of her bravery. She proclaimed God's command to Barak with confidence, emphasizing that success in battle depended not on human strength but on divine intervention. Her steadfast faith inspired those around her, proving that leadership rooted in spiritual conviction can overcome any obstacle.

Today's leaders can draw immense strength from Deborah's example. In moments of fear or uncertainty, remembering her unwavering faith can bolster our courage and remind us to rely on God's promises.

BARAK AND DEBORAH'S COLLABORATION

Barak and Deborah's partnership exemplifies the power of collaboration and mutual trust. Their complementary strengths, Barak's military expertise, and Deborah's prophetic wisdom, were essential in their victory against Sisera.

Their successful alliance also reveals the significance of unity and teamwork in achieving a common goal. Together, they rallied the tribes of Israel and united them towards a shared purpose. In doing so, they demonstrated that true leadership is not about individual accomplishment but about bringing people together towards a greater cause.

Barak's initial reluctance to lead the battle without Deborah's presence highlights a significant aspect of leadership—acknowledging one's limitations and seeking support. His hesitation was not a sign of weakness but an honest recognition of his need for Deborah's spiritual guidance and assurance.

This interaction underscores the importance of humility in leadership. By requesting Deborah's accompaniment, Barak demonstrated that true leaders are not afraid to seek help and collaborate with others to achieve a common goal. His willingness to rely on Deborah's faith and wisdom brought God's promise to fruition.

Deborah's response to Barak's request was one of encouragement and partnership. She agreed to accompany him, reinforcing the concept of collaborative leadership. Their joint effort was crucial in rallying the troops and boosting morale, leading to a decisive victory.

Deborah's encouragement illustrates the power of supportive leadership. Her willingness to stand by Barak, even in the face of potential danger, exemplifies the strength of unified effort. In today's context, leaders who foster teamwork and provide encouragement can inspire their teams to achieve remarkable outcomes.

The Benefits and Challenges of this Strategic Partnership

In reflecting upon the profound partnership between Barak and Deborah, we uncover a tapestry rich with both benefits and challenges that carry significant relevance for our contemporary lives.

- **The Benefits:** The benefits of their collaboration are striking; together, they achieved a unity of purpose that transcended their individual capabilities. This synergy not only brought forth a decisive victory against Sisera, but also fostered a community spirit among the tribes of Israel. In our own lives, cultivating partnerships where complementary strengths are recognized can lead to remarkable achievements, both personally and collectively. Embracing the diversity of talents and perspectives within a team can illuminate pathways to innovation and inspire collective resilience.

- **The Challenges:** However, the challenges inherent in this partnership cannot be overlooked. Barak's initial hesitation to act without Deborah highlights the vulnerability that comes with relying on another. It serves as a reminder that while collaboration can bear fruit, it may also reveal our insecurities and fears. Navigating such dynamics requires us to foster open communication and cultivate a culture of trust, where individuals feel safe to express their uncertainties. The key lies in embracing our limitations and being willing to lean on one another in moments of doubt, transforming vulnerability into a source of strength.

To navigate these intricate dynamics and foster growth and mutual success, we must actively cultivate an environment of empathy and shared vision. Encouraging honest dialogue and creating spaces where all voices are heard can significantly enhance collaborative efforts. Drawing inspiration from Deborah's supportive leadership, we can strive to uplift and empower those around us. By recognizing the value of each person's contribution and fostering a sense of belonging, we enrich the fabric of our relationships. Ultimately, embodying the spirit of unity and collaboration that Barak and Deborah exemplified can lead us towards a more harmonious and prosperous path, awakening the limitless potential within ourselves and our communities.

LESSONS FOR TODAY'S LEADERS

Deborah and Barak's partnership shows that true leadership goes beyond individual strengths, gender, or societal norms. It is about the willingness to trust in a higher purpose and collaborate with others towards a shared goal. Their story serves as an enduring example of courage, faith, and unity in the face of adversity.

As we navigate our own paths, may we draw inspiration from Deborah's leadership and strive to lead with compassion, conviction, and an unwavering belief in God's promises. May we also remember the power of collaboration and teamwork in overcoming any obstacle that comes our way. In doing so, we can leave behind a legacy that will continue to inspire generations to come.

Inspiration from Deborah and Barak

The story of Deborah and Barak is rich with profound lessons that resonate with contemporary leaders across various fields. Firstly, Deborah's example serves as a powerful reminder of the critical importance of recognizing and empowering female leaders. In a world where gender bias often persists, her story illustrates that true leadership is defined not by gender but by character, competence, and the ability to inspire others. Deborah's leadership in a male-dominated society teaches us that inclusion and diversity are essential for fostering innovation and growth.

Secondly, Barak's willingness to seek Deborah's support emphasizes the invaluable nature of collaboration in leadership. His acknowledgment of the need for Deborah's insights showcases the importance of humility and the recognition that no leader has all the answers. By actively seeking diverse perspectives and leveraging the unique strengths of their team members, leaders can make more informed decisions that consider various angles and experiences. This approach not only leads to more effective leadership but also cultivates a culture of trust and collaboration within organizations. Ultimately, the partnership between Deborah and Barak exemplifies how strong, inclusive leadership can pave the way for success in any endeavor.

The Value of Courage and Inclusivity

Courage is a fundamental quality in leadership, as vividly illustrated by the inspiring figures of Deborah and Barak. Their faith-driven bravery in the face of overwhelming odds serves as a powerful reminder that effective leaders must often take bold steps, trusting in a higher purpose and their vision. This kind of courage not only empowers leaders to face challenges head-on but also inspires their teams to push beyond their limits. It encourages a culture where taking calculated risks is seen as a pathway to growth and success.

Inclusivity is another critical lesson that emerges from their leadership journey. Deborah's remarkable ability to challenge and break societal norms was a groundbreaking move, paving the way for future generations of female leaders to follow in her footsteps. By promoting inclusivity and actively recognizing the contributions of all individuals—regardless of gender, background, or perspective—leaders can build more dynamic and innovative organizations. Embracing diverse viewpoints leads to richer discussions, more creative solutions, and ultimately, a stronger, more resilient team capable of navigating the complexities of today's world. Through courage and inclusivity, leaders can cultivate environments where everyone feels valued and empowered to contribute their best.

Reliance on God

Above all, the story of Deborah and Barak underscores the importance of relying on God in all aspects of leadership. Their success was not solely due to their abilities, strategic planning, or military tactics but to their unwavering faith and obedience to God's commands. Deborah, as a prophetess and judge, exemplified the power of divine guidance, while Barak showcased the strength that comes from trusting in God's promise.

In today's fast-paced and often chaotic world, modern leaders can draw immense strength and guidance from their relationship with God. By openly engaging with God, leaders can develop a deeper understanding of His will while exemplifying the strength of a Godly relationship. This spiritual foundation allows them to navigate challenges with confidence, trusting that He will provide wisdom and support in every endeavor. Ultimately, relying on God not only enhances personal leadership but also inspires those around them to seek higher purposes and values in their own lives.

THE STORY of Deborah and Barak stands as a powerful testament to the effectiveness of collaborative leadership. Their partnership played a crucial role in delivering Israel from Canaanite oppression. Deborah, as a prophetess and leader, provided wisdom and guidance, while Barak, a military commander, brought his strategic military acumen to the battlefield. This narrative serves as a reminder that leadership is not a solitary endeavor; it thrives on the synergy of diverse talents and perspectives, each contributing uniquely to the greater good.

In the context of modern leadership, the ability to collaborate and build cohesive teams is invaluable. Successful leaders recognize that fostering an environment where different strengths are harnessed towards a common objective not only enhances problem-solving but also drives innovation and creativity. By embracing a collaborative approach, leaders can create a culture of inclusivity and engagement, empowering team members to share their ideas and insights freely. This collective effort can lead to far greater success than any individual could achieve alone, underscoring the importance of collaboration in navigating today's complex challenges. Ultimately, the story of Deborah and Barak serves as an enduring inspiration for leaders seeking to cultivate teamwork and unity in pursuit of shared goals.

NEHEMIAH AND THE PEOPLE OF JERUSALEM

WE'RE BUILDING A WALL AND WE CAN'T COME DOWN

*N*ehemiah 4:6

In a time when Jerusalem lay in ruins, one man's leadership ignited a movement that transformed a broken city into a fortified haven. Nehemiah's story is one of remarkable resilience, collective effort, and unwavering faith. Set against the backdrop of the 5th century BCE, Nehemiah's return to Jerusalem occurred during a period of great uncertainty and vulnerability. The city walls had been torn down, leaving its inhabitants exposed to external threats and internal despair.

Nehemiah, a cupbearer to the Persian King Artaxerxes, was deeply moved by the plight of his people. His heart ached for Jerusalem, and he sought permission to return and rebuild the city. King Artaxerxes agreed and Nehemiah embarked upon his mission. Despite facing opposition and criticism, Nehemiah's unwavering determination to rebuild Jerusalem inspired others to join him in this monumental task.

THE STORY

As the golden sun dipped below the rugged hills surrounding Jerusalem, its warm glow enveloped the city, casting long shadows over the remains of crumbled stones and broken dreams. The air was thick with the scent of baked earth, mingling with the distant echoes of laughter and sorrow. Nehemiah, a cupbearer turned visionary leader, stood at the threshold of this ancient city, his heart pulsating with a fervent desire to restore not just the physical structures, but the very spirit of his people.

Gathered within the remnants of the once-great walls, a diverse assembly of artisans, farmers, and families infused with a profound sense of purpose filled the air. Each individual, regardless of their background, shared an unspoken bond—their shared hopes and dreams shimmering like stars in the twilight sky. With every whispered prayer and fervent vow, they embarked on a collective journey, igniting the embers of unity that had long been overshadowed by despair.

Nehemiah, fueled by divine inspiration, spoke passionately of their shared mission, laying out a vision reminiscent of a time where the the threads of resilience, faith, and determination were woven with eternal purpose. With hands raised and hearts open, they began their labor —a harmonious dance of movement, effort, and faith. The sound of chiseling stones and the rhythmic pounding of hammers reverberated like a sacred song through the valleys, as each brick they placed was a testament to their tenacity.

In the heart of the city, families worked side by side, their laughter ringing out like bells of celebration. Parents shielded little ones as they relocated stones, each child learning the importance of duty, hard work, and the power of faith. As the walls rose higher, so did the spirits of every builder, symbolizing a burgeoning strength that transcended mere construction—it was a revival of faith in themselves, their city, and in one another. Fear found no shelter here, for every challenge was met with encouragement, every lack with generosity, each setback met with a determination woven into the very fabric of their being.

As twilight turned to dawn, their collective effort birthed the beginnings of a renewed and mighty fortress, each wall standing as both a defense against external threats and a gentle reminder of the sanctity of community, and the faithfulness of God. Day by day, the walls became a beacon of hope, reflecting the vibrant hues of the sunrise and the dreams of those who dared to believe in a brighter future. Nehemiah was not merely a leader; he became the heart of a movement that starkly contrasted against the flickering shadows of doubt.

Through their unwavering commitment, the People of Jerusalem transformed their shared struggle into a strategic partnership, cultivating relationships that fostered healing and hope. Each brick laid was a heartbeat for the city, and each shared moment of labour was a step toward reclaiming their identity. In the end, it wasn't just the walls that were rebuilt; it was the very essence of Jerusalem—a living testament to the power of unity and the divine spark within each heart.

THE BENEFITS AND CHALLENGES OF STRATEGIC PARTNERSHIP

In the delicate dance of collaboration exemplified by Nehemiah and the People of Jerusalem, we uncover rich lessons that resonate profoundly in our current reality. At the heart of strategic partnerships is the immense value of unity nurtured through shared goals and mutual trust. Such alliances invite diverse talents and perspectives, weaving a rich tapestry of ideas that fosters innovation and creativity. Each participant, imbued with their unique gifts, contributes to a collective powerhouse, multiplying the potential for success. This spirit of togetherness enables us to tackle challenges with resilience and grace, finding strength in solidarity—a reminder that no one need bear their burdens alone.

However, forging and maintaining these partnerships is not without its challenges. Differing motivations, communication barriers, and the inevitability of external pressures can strain relationships and hinder progress. It is in these moments of discord that we must remember the essence of compassion and understanding. To navigate these dynamics, embracing an open dialogue is paramount; actively listening to one another fosters empathy and reveals the underlying needs that often fuel conflict.

Regular reflections on shared values and aspirations can realign intentions, creating a nurturing space where growth thrives.

As Nehemiah stood resolute against his oppressors, a fiery spirit ignited within him, compelling him to declare, "I'm building a wall and I can't come down." In that pivotal moment, he demonstrated his unwavering determination in the task at hand, knowing that words alone would not restore his people's hope. The time for dialogue had dissolved, replaced by the urgency of action. Nehemiah grasped his trowel in one hand, a symbol of his commitment to create new beginnings, while his other hand gripped a sword, representing the necessity to protect and defend their divine mission. This intimate duality of construction and combat illustrates the reality that, often, we are called to build even amidst adversity.

The adversities surrounding him did not diminish his resolve; instead, they crystallized it. In the face of taunts and threats, he rallied his people, urging them to embrace their roles as both builders and defenders. The path forward demanded that they cultivate both strength and faith, recognizing that the time to act is NOW. They could not afford to wait for this battle to pass; they were to rise with resilience, facing each challenge head-on while laying the foundation of their mission.

This profound truth resonates deeply with us—there are moments in our own lives when we must balance the act of building our futures while bravely confronting the trials that seek to hinder us. Fueled by faith and determination, we can embark on the noble pursuit of building and overcoming challenges, persevering through hardship to achieve our assignments, even in the face of adversity.

A CLOSER LOOK AT COLLECTIVE RESILIENCE

The verse Nehemiah 4 6 states,

> "We rebuilt the wall till all of it reached half its height, for the people worked with all their heart."

This simple yet profound scripture encapsulates the essence of collective resilience. Despite facing opposition and threats from surrounding enemies, the people of Jerusalem united with a shared purpose. Their unwavering determination and communal effort enabled them to achieve what seemed impossible.

Nehemiah 4 6 teaches us the power of working together with a common goal. The people of Jerusalem didn't just rebuild a wall; they restored their sense of security, dignity, and hope. This act of unity is a testament to what can be accomplished when individuals come together, pooling their strengths and resources for a greater cause.

In our modern world, the concept of collective resilience remains as relevant as ever. Whether facing personal hardships, professional setbacks, or global crises, working together with a shared purpose can lead to extraordinary outcomes. Nehemiah 4 6 reminds us that resilience is not just an individual trait but a communal strength.

Building Collective Resilience

Building collective resilience in today's world requires intentional efforts in community building, leadership, and problem-solving. Here are some actionable steps to help foster this resilience:

Community Building:

- Create spaces for open dialogue and mutual support.
- Community centers, online forums, and local gatherings can serve as platforms for sharing experiences and resources.
- Encourage collaboration by organizing community projects that address shared challenges. These projects can range from neighborhood clean-ups to advocacy campaigns for social justice.

Leadership:

- Adopt a servant leadership approach, prioritizing the needs and well-being of the community. Leaders should inspire trust and motivate others through empathy and transparency.
- Establish clear goals and communicate them effectively. A shared vision helps align

individual efforts towards a common purpose, fostering a sense of unity.

Problem-Solving:

- Promote a culture of innovation and adaptability. Encourage community members to contribute ideas and solutions, and be open to new approaches.
- Provide training and resources to enhance problem-solving skills. Workshops, webinars, and mentorship programs can equip individuals with the tools they need to address challenges effectively.

By implementing these strategies, communities can strengthen their collective resilience, creating a supportive environment where individuals thrive together.

LESSONS FROM NEHEMIAH'S LEADERSHIP

Nehemiah's leadership was characterized by vision, faith, strategy, and empathy. He understood the gravity of the situation and motivated the people with a clear and compelling vision. Nehemiah's strategic approach included assessing the damage, delegating tasks, and organizing the workforce efficiently. His empathy shone through in his genuine concern for the people's well-being and his ability to inspire them to work with all their heart.

One of Nehemiah's key strategies was to assign specific sections of the wall to different families and groups. This not only ensured accountability but also fostered a sense of ownership and pride in the work. Each group knew that their contribution was vital to the overall success of the project.

Nehemiah also prioritized communication and transparency. He kept the people informed about the progress and the challenges they faced, which helped maintain morale and trust. His leadership style was not authoritarian but collaborative, encouraging everyone to contribute their best efforts.

These lessons from Nehemiah's leadership are timeless. Today's leaders can draw inspiration from his approach to build resilient teams and communities. By fostering a clear vision, strategic planning, empathy, and effective communication, leaders can unite people towards achieving common goals, even in the face of adversity.

THE IMPORTANCE OF STRATEGIC PARTNERSHIP

The partnership between Nehemiah and the people of Jerusalem is a powerful example of how individuals and leaders can work together to overcome adversity. Here are some key takeaways from their partnership:

- **The Importance of Leadership in Times of Challenge**

In moments of adversity, the essence of true leadership shines most brightly. Nehemiah's steadfast guidance during the reconstruction of Jerusalem's walls exemplifies how effective leadership plays a crucial role in navigating the turbulent waters of challenge. He not only set a clear vision but also empowered each individual to embrace their unique contributions, reminding them of their significance in the collective effort. In times of strife, leaders must possess the wisdom to encourage their teams to "stay in their own lane," harnessing their strengths while trusting in the direction provided.

By focusing on individual responsibilities within the grander scheme, team members cultivate a sense of purpose and fulfillment. Nehemiah understood this balance; he delegated tasks thoughtfully, allowing each household to take ownership of specific sections of the wall. This approach not only nurtured accountability but built a deep sense of connection among the people. In a world filled with uncertainty, the need for compassionate and clear leadership cannot be overstated. Leaders must foster an environment of trust where direction is given with love, encouraging all to contribute wholeheartedly while supporting one another. Together, we can navigate the challenges we face, building stronger foundations for the futures we envision.

- **The Importance of Perseverance Amidst Turmoil**

The journey of rebuilding the wall under Nehemiah's leadership stands as a profound testament to the strength of perseverance in the face of adversity. During a time of conflict and uncertainty, Nehemiah and the people of Jerusalem understood that their vision could not afford to be derailed by the chaos surrounding them. Instead of halting their progress due to the threats that loomed, they chose to confront their challenges with courage and unwavering resolve. This act of moving forward, even amidst a battle, is a powerful reminder that progress is not merely a result of external circumstances but is deeply rooted in our commitment to a shared purpose.

Just as Nehemiah rallied his people to work diligently while remaining vigilant against opposition, we too can find inspiration in their dedication. When we encounter struggles—whether in our personal lives or within our communities—it is essential to keep our eyes on our goals and continue to labour with intention and faith. The walls we build are not just physical structures; they represent our hopes, dreams, and resilience. By embracing the challenges we face and persevering through them, we honor the spirit of collective effort, ensuring that our work resonates beyond the tumultuous times. Together, we can forge ahead, nurturing strength and unity, refusing to let conflict diminish our vision for a brighter future.

- **The Importance of Handling People Correctly**

In the journey of rebuilding both walls and relationships, the way we handle the individuals around us profoundly impacts the outcomes we achieve. Nehemiah's leadership instinctively embraced a philosophy founded on encouragement, instruction, and empathy for his people, allowing their spirits to soar even amidst adversity. By providing clear guidance and heartfelt encouragement, leaders can nurture resilience within their teams, helping each member feel valued and empowered. Just as Nehemiah's people found strength in collective support, so too can we foster an environment where everyone is uplifted, encouraging cooperation and unity in purpose.

Conversely, the taunting enemies that sought to undermine their efforts were met with rebuke and diminishment. This vital contrast teaches us the importance of choosing our battles wisely; standing firm against negativity and derision fosters a healthier and more encouraging atmosphere for growth. The moral here echoes with profound significance:

As we navigate the relationships within our lives, let us be drawn to encouragement and support, while firmly rejecting those that seek to diminish our potential. By consciously choosing to empower those around us and rising above adversity, we can create a legacy marked by resilience, compassion, and the unwavering pursuit of a brighter future together.

CONCLUSION AND CALL TO ACTION

Nehemiah's remarkable story of rebuilding Jerusalem's walls amidst substantial adversity serves as a powerful testament to the strength that can be found in communal purpose and resilience. His unwavering leadership, the unity exhibited by the people, and the real-world examples of collective resilience not only highlight the importance of teamwork but also provide valuable insights that resonate with the challenges we face today.

Throughout history, we have seen how communities come together to overcome obstacles, whether through grassroots movements, local initiatives, or simply by supporting one another during difficult times. Nehemiah's experience reminds us that even when the odds seem insurmountable, a shared vision and determination can lead to extraordinary outcomes.

Let me invite you to take a moment to reflect on your own experiences of collective resilience. How have you witnessed or actively contributed to overcoming challenges through your efforts? Whether its a neighborhood coming together to support a family in need, a team uniting to tackle a daunting project, or a community rallying around a cause, your insights can inspire and empower others. Join the conversation and help amplify the message of strength and unity that we can all draw upon.

As we look to the future, may Nehemiah's story continue to inspire us to build stronger, more resilient communities, grounded in faith, collaboration, and shared purpose. Together, we possess the ability to achieve remarkable things, transforming challenges into opportunities for growth and connection. Let's unite in our efforts and make a meaningful impact for Christ in our world today!

ESTHER AND MORDECAI

COURAGE UNDER FIRE

*E*sther 4:13-14
In the lush, sun-drenched kingdom of Persia, where the aromas of spices danced through markets filled with vibrant fabrics and bustling voices, a profound story of bravery and faith unfolded. This realm, ruled by King Xerxes, was abundant in wealth but starkly contrasting in its governance. It was within these opulent palaces, adorned with gold and surrounded by envious courtiers, that a humble yet striking young woman named Esther emerged. With her piercing eyes, full of dreams, and a heart that pulsed with compassion, she had ascended from her Jewish roots to become queen, a beacon of unyielding strength amid the shadows of despair.

But this was no fairy tale; it was a time of great peril, as a scheming minister named Haman plotted the annihilation of the Jewish people. Shadows loomed large, threatening to engulf the very fabric of their existence.

Mordecai, Esther's steadfast guardian and uncle, whose wisdom lay as thick as the Persian silk around them, sensed the machine of destruction raging in the distance. With a heart heavy yet resolute, he brought word to Esther, urging her to embrace her royal position and advocate for her people.

"Do not think that you will escape the fate of all the Jews," he implored, his voice laced with both urgency and love, "for perhaps it is for such a time as this that you have come to your royal position." Underneath the vast canopy of the starlit sky, amidst whispers of concern and the rustling leaves, a pact formed between them—a sacred partnership emblazoned on the strings of destiny.

Esther, her spirit ignited by Mordecai's unwavering faith, adorned herself in regal splendor, draping herself in the finest silk, her attire shimmering like the morning sun breaking through the darkness. With each step she took into the opulent courts of the king, she moved with the grace of a lioness, despite the tempest of uncertainty within. Her mind raced with thoughts of her people, hurtling toward a brink from which there was no return.

Gathering her courage, she crafted a banquet—a feast that would entice the king, a moment spun with purpose and strategy. As the guests reclined, cushioned in luxurious velvet, Esther unveiled her truth, her voice a clear, melodious tide against the shifting currents of dread.

> "If I have found favor in your eyes, O King, spare my life and the lives of my people!"

she cried, her words weaving a tapestry of urgency that enveloped the hall.

The room fell silent, the air heavy with disbelief, as the king's attention was captured. Through Esther's strength and Mordecai's unwavering support, a revolution of hope flourished within the corridors of power. The truth unraveled the threads of deception, revealing Haman's treachery, the evil plot dissolving like sugar in water. Esther's bravery illuminated the path for her people, a testament to the power of faith, love and solidarity that transcends the boundaries of fear.

In the aftermath, as the stars twinkled brightly above the kingdom, celebrating the dawn of freedom, a newfound spirit of unity blossomed. Esther and Mordecai's strategic partnership had not only salvaged lives but had sown seeds of resilience that would endure throughout generations. Their story, rich with the vibrancy of culture, echoing through ages, teaches us of the indomitable power of courage, compassion, and unwavering faith in unity's embrace against the tides of adversity. Through their legacy, we are reminded that in the darkest of times, the light of love, and faith in a God who does not fail, will always guide us home.

ESTHER AND MORDECAI'S INDIVIDUAL COURAGE

While Esther and Mordecai's partnership was an essential factor in their triumph over adversity, it is also crucial to recognize the individual courage they both displayed.

Despite living in a society where women and minorities were often marginalized, Esther spoke up and took action for her people without hesitation. She risked her own life by approaching the king uninvited, breaking societal norms and defying the fear that threatened to consume her.

Mordecai, on the other hand, showed immense bravery by standing up against Haman, a man of great power and influence. He refused to bow down to him, even at the cost of his own safety. His unwavering faith in God gave him strength to persevere, and his quick thinking and wisdom ultimately led to the downfall of their enemy.

Their individual acts of courage complemented each other, creating a powerful force that could not be defeated. Together, they showed us that even in the face of great adversity, it is possible to find strength in God as we stand up for what is right.

ESTHER'S JOURNEY FROM ORPHAN TO QUEEN

Esther's transformation from an orphaned Jewish girl to the queen of Persia is nothing short of miraculous. Her elevation to royalty wasn't merely a twist of fate; it was a divine appointment that set the stage for a greater purpose. Despite the immense challenges and risks, Esther's courage shines through as she embraces her newfound role with grace and wisdom.

Living in the palace, Esther had to hide her Jewish identity on Mordecai's advice. Her life of luxury could have distanced her from her people's plight, but Esther's heart remained with them. Her bold decision to approach King Xerxes, uninvited, to plead for her people's lives, exemplifies her profound bravery and selflessness.

This powerful lesson reminds us that regardless of how far God elevates us, we must never forget our roots. Our humble beginnings serve as a reminder of the struggles we have overcome and keep us grounded in our faith and compassion for others.

MORDECAI'S FAITH AND STRATEGIC THINKING

Mordecai's wise counsel and unwavering faith in God played a significant role in the events that unfolded. Despite the grave danger they faced, he refused to compromise his beliefs or bow down to Haman. His strategic thinking also proved vital when he urged Esther to reveal her identity at just the right time, leading to their enemy's downfall.

His example teaches us that even in the midst of uncertainty, we must hold fast to our faith and trust in God's plan. It is through His guidance that we can find wisdom and discernment to navigate through life's challenges.

The story of Esther and Mordecai is a testament to the power of courage, faith, and unity in the face of adversity. Their partnership serves as an inspiration for us all, reminding us that when we stand together with unwavering faith in God, nothing can stop us from overcoming even the greatest challenges.

THE CRUCIAL PARTNERSHIP OF ESTHER AND MORDECAI

The partnership between Esther and Mordecai was a beacon of hope for the Jewish people during one of their darkest times. Their complementary strengths and deep mutual trust enabled them to confront the perilous challenges that threatened their very existence. Mordecai's wisdom and strategic guidance, drawn from his experiences and understanding of the political landscape, coupled with Esther's elevated royal position and remarkable bravery, created a formidable alliance. Together, they navigated the intricacies of court life and the looming threat of annihilation, ultimately leading their people toward salvation.

In Esther 4:13-14, Mordecai's poignant words to Esther encapsulate the essence of their partnership. He reminds her that her royal position may have been divinely orchestrated,

> "for such a time as this,"

urging her to act with courage and unwavering faith. This powerful call to action ignites a spark in Esther, motivating her to step beyond her comfort zone and take risks for the sake of her people. It is this moment of decisive intervention that not only showcases her courage but also highlights the critical importance of their partnership in overcoming adversity. The collaboration between Esther and Mordecai demonstrates that true strength lies in unity, trust, and the willingness to fight for what is right, even in the face of overwhelming odds.

LESSONS IN LEADERSHIP AND PARTNERSHIP

The story of Esther and Mordecai exemplifies powerful lessons in leadership and partnership that are applicable even in modern times. Their unwavering faith in God provided them with the courage, wisdom, and discernment to navigate through difficult circumstances. Their partnership serves as a reminder that when we come together with a common purpose, trusting in each other's strengths, we can overcome any challenge.

Their example also teaches us the importance of standing up for what is right, even if it means going against societal norms or risking our own safety. And most importantly, their story shows us that no matter how dark and dire the situation may seem, there is always hope and salvation when we put our trust in God.

STRATEGIC ALLIANCES IN TIMES OF CHALLENGE

The story of Esther and Mordecai underscores the necessity of strategic alliances in navigating crises. Their partnership was built on a foundation of shared values, a deep sense of purpose, and a common goal—the preservation of their people during a time of great peril. This historical narrative highlights the importance of collaboration and collective action, which can provide a roadmap for modern leaders facing their own challenges.

In today's complex world, leaders can draw valuable insights from the dynamic between Esther and Mordecai. They recognized that effective partnerships are not only beneficial but essential in overcoming significant obstacles. This collaboration exemplifies how shared objectives can unite individuals, fostering a sense of community and resilience.

Effective partnerships require clear communication, unwavering trust, and a willingness to leverage each other's strengths. Just as Esther and Mordecai combined their unique abilities, with Esther's courage and Mordecai's wisdom, to achieve a greater good, contemporary leaders can benefit from forging alliances that amplify their impact. By pooling resources, perspectives, and expertise, they can drive collective success and navigate the complexities of modern challenges more effectively. In times of crisis, it is this unity and collaboration that can ultimately lead to triumph and growth, both for individuals and for the communities they serve.

COURAGE AND WISDOM FOR THE GREATER GOOD... FROM GOD

Courage and wisdom are indispensable qualities for any leader, serving as the foundation for effective and ethical decision-making. The biblical narrative of Esther and Mordecai beautifully exemplifies these vital attributes. Esther's remarkable bravery in approaching the king, risking her own safety to advocate for her people, combined with Mordecai's strategic foresight and unwavering support, played a crucial role in averting disaster and ensuring the survival of the Jewish community. Their story serves as a powerful reminder that true leadership often involves making difficult decisions and taking bold actions for the benefit of others, even in the face of adversity.

Leaders today can look to Esther and Mordecai as inspirational figures, emulating their qualities by cultivating courage and wisdom in their own lives and leadership styles. This means standing up for what is right, even when it is unpopular or fraught with risk. It requires the ability to navigate complex situations with integrity and the willingness to challenge the status quo. Furthermore, it involves actively seeking divine guidance through prayer and reflection, as well as relying on the collective wisdom of others to make informed and impactful decisions. By doing so, leaders can not only foster a supportive environment but also inspire those around them to act with courage and wisdom for the greater good.

PRACTICAL APPLICATION FOR MODERN READERS

The story of Esther and Mordecai may have taken place thousands of years ago, but the lessons it teaches are timeless. In today's world, where leadership and partnership are more critical than ever, we can look to this biblical narrative for guidance on how to navigate through crises with grace, wisdom, and faith.

In our personal lives, we can draw inspiration from Esther and Mordecai's example by fostering strong, supportive relationships. Identify those in your life who share your values and vision, and work together to achieve common goals. Whether it's within your family, friends, or community, cultivating partnerships based on trust and mutual respect can lead to meaningful and impactful outcomes.

When faced with challenges, remember Esther's courage by stepping out of your comfort zone and taking decisive action. Seek wisdom and guidance from trusted advisors, just as Esther leaned on Mordecai's counsel. Remember, you are never alone in your struggles—lean on God and your Christian community for support and encouragement.

For business professionals and organizational leaders, the story of Esther and Mordecai offers timeless leadership lessons. Successful leadership often involves balancing courage with wisdom, making strategic decisions that serve the greater good, and building strong alliances.

Encourage open communication and collaboration within your teams. Recognize and leverage the unique strengths of each individual, fostering a culture of mutual respect and shared purpose. When challenges arise, approach them with a combination of bold action and thoughtful strategy, just as Esther and Mordecai did.

Faith-based communities can also benefit from the

lessons of Esther and Mordecai. By fostering a sense of unity and collective purpose, these groups can overcome challenges and drive positive change. Encourage members to support one another, share their experiences, and work together towards common goals.

Promote open dialogue and active participation within your community. Create opportunities for members to collaborate on projects, share their talents, and contribute to the greater good. By emulating the partnership of Esther and Mordecai, faith-based groups can build stronger, more resilient communities.

THE STORY of Esther and Mordecai is a powerful testament to the importance of courage, wisdom, and strategic partnerships. Their unwavering faith and determination not only saved their people but also left a lasting legacy of leadership and collaboration.

As we reflect on their story, let's strive to embody these qualities in our own lives. Whether in personal relationships, professional settings, or faith-based communities, the lessons of Esther and Mordecai can guide us towards greater resilience, unity, and impact.

PAUL AND BARNABAS

A DIVINELY APPOINTED PARTNERSHIP

*A*cts 13:2-3

In the bustling heart of Antioch, where the aroma of spices mingled with the fervent chants of worship, two souls were destined to intertwine in a divine tapestry of purpose. Paul, once a zealous adversary of the nascent Christian faith, had undergone a radical transformation on the road to Damascus. His heart ignited with a fervor that echoed the very heartbeat of God and His desire to reach humanity, Paul sought to share the gospel with fervent passion. In contrast, Barnabas, son of encouragement, was renowned for his unwavering kindness and keen insight into the human spirit. It was through Barnabas's compassionate embrace and willingness to see the potential where others saw failure that Paul found his footing among the brethren, his past washed away like the morning dew.

As whispers of their vibrant ministry spread through

the cobbled streets of Antioch, the community gathered, a richly woven tapestry of cultures and backgrounds. Jew and Gentile alike found their hearts stirred by the bold proclamations of these two men, who spoke as vessels of hope amidst a society desperately longing for light. The synagogue became a sanctuary of spirited dialogue, while the open squares pulsed with the rhythmic footfalls of seekers yearning for truth. Together, Paul and Barnabas brought forth a symphony of faith, their voices harmonizing the old prophecies with the unfolding story of Jesus, the Messiah, whose love knew no bounds.

One fateful day, as the atmosphere brimmed with reverence, the Holy Spirit stirred within the hearts of the prophets and teachers. In the stillness of their gathering, a divine commission was birthed, calling Paul and Barnabas to set sail for the distant shores of Cyprus and beyond, where the gospel awaited to penetrate the hearts of the unknowing. With the blessing of the church, they embarked on their journey, sails billowing against a brilliant azure sky, a metaphorical voyage that mirrored their spiritual odyssey.

As they traversed rocky terrain and vibrant ports, the duo encountered both adversities and blessings that tested their resolve. In the lush groves of Cyprus, the vivid hues of the land contrasted starkly with the shadows of doubt they faced. Their relentless spirit shone brightly before the proconsul, Sergius Paulus, a man of intellect yearning for enlightenment. With the grace of missionaries and the fervor of prophets, they challenged the darkness represented by Elymas, the sorcerer, proclaiming the truth with unwavering authority. The clash was not merely physical; it was a battle for the hearts and minds of the people. As the sun dipped low on the horizon, the light of understanding flooded over Sergius, illuminating his soul, bringing forth the beauty of belief.

Through stony paths and bustling marketplaces, the vibrant tapestry of Paul and Barnabas's partnership unfurled, weaving their spirits together as they engaged with diverse cultures and hearts hungry for truth. Their journey reflected the essence of compassion, as they embraced each individual, speaking words of love and life. Each town they visited became a canvas upon which they painted an enduring legacy, leaving behind not merely the message of Jesus, but also the salt and light of their friendship, a testament to how unity in purpose not only empowers the messenger but enriches the message itself.

In an age marked by strife and despair, the story of Paul and Barnabas serves as a luminous reminder of the transformative power of partnership, compassion, and faith. Their divinely appointed journey illuminated the way for countless seekers and speaks to us still, echoing through the ages like a melody that whispers, "You are never alone on the path of purpose."

The Context of Acts 13:2-3

Acts 13:2-3 serves as a pivotal moment in the New Testament. It marks the start of Paul and Barnabas's first missionary journey, a venture that would spread the Gospel far and wide. The verses state,

> "While they were worshiping the Lord and fasting, the Holy Spirit said, 'Set apart for me Barnabas and Saul for the work to which I have called them.' Then after fasting and praying, they laid their hands on them and sent them off."

This passage is rich in context and meaning. It highlights a community engaged in worship and fasting, creating an environment where the Holy Spirit could clearly communicate. The selection of Paul and Barnabas was not a human decision but a divine appointment, emphasizing the importance of spiritual discernment in leadership.

THE JOURNEYS OF PAUL AND BARNABAS

The journeys of Paul and Barnabas were not merely travels across the land; they were sacred pilgrimages, carving pathways for the New Testament Church to flourish amidst diverse cultures and challenges. As they ventured through regions such as Cyprus, Pisidia, and Lycaonia, their unwavering commitment to sharing the gospel ignited a fire that would influence countless hearts and communities. In Acts 14:21-22, we see their resolve manifest as they retraced their steps to strengthen the souls of the disciples, encouraging them to persevere in the faith while reminding them,

> "Through many tribulations we must enter the kingdom of God."

This profound encouragement, underpinned by compassion, instilled hope in the believers, empowering them to withstand these trials.

In each city, they proclaimed the good news, and the impact was palpable. Acts 13:48 reveals the fruits of their labour as it recounts how

> *"when the Gentiles heard this, they began rejoicing and glorifying the word of the Lord, and as many as were appointed to eternal life believed."*

This shift towards inclusivity, embracing Gentiles into the fold of Christ, was monumental in establishing a diverse yet unified body of believers. The transformation in places like Iconium (Acts 14:1) demonstrated their ability to bridge cultural divides, fostering churches that were vibrant expressions of faith that transcended previously-held boundaries.

Their journeys also ignited discussions that shaped the very doctrine of the Church. The encounter in Acts 15 at the Council of Jerusalem stands as a crucial moment where they defended the necessity of grace over law, affirming the salvation offered through Jesus Christ alone. It was through this compassionate dialogue that they helped define core tenets of faith, steering the Church towards a future grounded in love, grace, and unity.

Thus, the journeys of Paul and Barnabas were woven into the very fabric of the New Testament Church, fostering growth, resilience, and a deep sense of purpose that echoes through the ages. They remind us of the transformative power of unity in mission and spirit, as they forged a legacy that continues to inspire believers to reach out, embrace, and serve the world with the message of hope and love.

Their friendship, rooted in shared faith and a deep sense of purpose, nurtured an environment where they could support one another through trials and challenges. In Acts 15:36-41, we see how even amidst their disagreement, they upheld each other's dignity and respect, choosing to part ways rather than engage in conflict that would hinder their mission.

Their vision for the Gospel united them as they navigated difficult terrains and cultures with compassion and grace. Their shared understanding of the Gospel message fueled their passion for evangelism, reorienting them towards the eternal significance of their calling. This focus on the enduring impact of their work enabled them to persevere through hardships with unwavering determination.

MUTUAL ENCOURAGEMENT, SHARED VISION, AND SPIRITUAL DIRECTION

The collaboration between Paul and Barnabas exemplifies the profound impact of mutual encouragement, shared vision, and spiritual guidance in their mission endeavors. These elements not only fortified their partnership but also illuminated a path for contemporary church leaders to follow.

Mutual Encouragement

The bond between Paul and Barnabas was deeply rooted in mutual encouragement. In times of trial and triumph, they were each other's pillars of strength, offering unwavering support and motivation. This mutual encouragement was not merely an exchange of kind words; it was a spiritual lifeline that helped them navigate the turbulent waters of their mission. For instance, when Paul faced opposition and persecution, Barnabas stood by him, reinforcing his resolve and reminding him of the divine purpose behind their struggles.

Today, this principle is vital in ministry. Leaders who encourage one another create a resilient and focused environment, where each member is uplifted and fortified against the challenges they face. Mutual encouragement fosters a community of faith that is robust, compassionate, and unwavering in its divine mission.

Shared Vision

Central to the collaboration between Paul and Barnabas was a shared vision. Their commitment to spreading the Gospel and establishing Christian communities was the unifying force that aligned their efforts. This shared vision enabled them to work cohesively and effectively, ensuring that every step they took was purposeful and aligned with their divine mission. For example, their journey to Cyprus and beyond was marked by a clear and unified goal: to bring the light of Christ to new lands and establish strong foundations for the early church.

In modern ministry, a shared vision is the cornerstone of effective teamwork. When leaders are united by a common purpose, their collaborative efforts are amplified, driving the mission forward with clarity and determination. A shared vision transforms a group of individuals into a harmonious and dynamic force for good, each contributing their unique gifts towards a greater divine purpose.

Spiritual Direction

The collaboration between Paul and Barnabas was profoundly guided by spiritual direction. They were attuned to the Holy Spirit, allowing divine guidance to steer their actions and decisions. This reliance on spiritual direction ensured that their ministry was not just a series of human efforts but a divinely orchestrated mission. An example of this can be seen in their decision to part ways for separate missions, a decision that was made after discerning the Holy Spirit's guidance. This allowed them to cover more ground and spread the Gospel even further.

For contemporary church leaders, spiritual direction is indispensable. By seeking and following divine guidance, leaders can make decisions that are aligned with God's will, ensuring that their ministry reflects the intentions of God Almighty. Spiritual direction provides a compass that helps leaders navigate the complexities of their mission with wisdom, humility, and unwavering faith.

In essence, the collaboration between Paul and Barnabas offers timeless insights into the power of mutual encouragement, shared vision, and spiritual direction. These elements are not just historical anecdotes but living principles that can transform modern ministry. By embracing mutual encouragement, leaders can foster resilience and strength within their communities. Through a shared vision, they can enhance teamwork and drive their mission forward with unity and purpose. And by seeking spiritual direction, they can ensure that their actions are in harmony with divine intentions, leading their communities with wisdom and grace. As we reflect on the legacy of Paul and Barnabas, may we be inspired to cultivate these principles in our own ministries, creating a tapestry of faith that is resilient, united, and divinely guided.

THE COLLABORATION of Paul and Barnabas in Acts 13 2-3 offers timeless lessons for church leaders and Christian ministries today. Their story highlights the importance of mutual encouragement, shared vision, and spiritual direction in achieving greater impact in ministry. By applying these principles, modern church leaders can foster effective collaboration and teamwork within their organizations, ensuring that their efforts are aligned with God's will and purpose.

In conclusion, the story of Paul and Barnabas is a powerful reminder of the significance of collaboration in ministry. Their partnership, guided by the Holy Spirit, achieved remarkable outcomes and set a precedent for future generations of Christian leaders. By prioritizing prayer, mutual support, shared vision, and spiritual direction, church leaders today can create a strong foundation for impactful ministry.

TIMOTHY AND PAUL

THE POWER OF MENTORSHIP

2 Timothy 1:5

In the vibrant early days of Christianity, a stirring alliance was born between two souls destined for greatness—Timothy, a young disciple whose heart burned with a passionate desire for truth, and Paul, the seasoned Apostle whose transformative zeal carried the weight of Godly wisdom. The landscape was rich with the colors of a world in flux; bustling markets filled with merchants bartering for wares, the melodies of laughter and debate echoing through the winding streets of cities like Ephesus and Corinth. Here, the very air tingled with the promise of change and the whisper of new beginnings.

Timothy, raised in a home where the gentle teachings of his grandmother Lois, and mother Eunice, shaped his spirit, found himself at a crossroads. Because of their influence he embraced the teachings of Christianity, but it was the fiery presence of the Apostle Paul that ignited a deeper longing within him—a longing to carry the light of the gospel into the shadowy corners of the world. With a heart full of ambition and questions, Timothy looked up to Paul as a spiritual father, a mentor who embodied the voice of the God, guiding him along his new found ministry path.

Paul, aware of the sacred charge bestowed upon him, recognized the spark within young Timothy. He took him by the hand (figuratively speaking) and led him into the bustling heart of their mission. At times the journey was treacherous, filled with challenges and trials and other times they enjoyed and celebrated the triumphs as together they witnessed the unexplainable hand of God like a brushstroke on the canvas of their ministry. They traversed mountains, crossed rivers, and navigated cities alive with chatter, as the sun cast golden rays upon their evangelistic and church-planting path path as God guided their quest.

Through vibrant dialogues over communal meals, beneath the starlit skies of night, and during fervent prayers that rose like incense into the heavens, the profound bond between Paul and Timothy blossomed as the Apostle Paul poured into his young mentee. Through stories of shipwrecks and imprisonments, and moments where faith stood as a fortress against the fiercest storms, Paul instilled in Timothy the understanding that such struggles were the very fabric of spiritual growth and maturity.

Timothy learned not only from Paul's teachings but also from his heart—a gentle compassion that echoed through every word of encouragement. With every step they took, Timothy grew not just in knowledge, but in strength and confidence, becoming a vessel through which grace would flow into the lives of others. The stories they crafted together became testaments of hope, woven into the lives of those who sought the light of gospel truth amid the darkness of doubt.

In this sacred partnership, the legacy of their faith journey began to unfurl, creating ripples that would traverse generations. Surely they sensed that the bond they nurtured was a reflection of the love of God that connected them to each other, and to the world. Timothy, emboldened by Paul's unwavering wisdom and support, was not just preparing to inherit a mission; he was poised to ignite a movement—a beautiful symphony of faith, resonating through the ages, inviting all to partake in the compassionate embrace of God's love.

As these two men embarked on their journey, the essence of their story pulsed vibrantly, embodying the profound impact of mentorship, faith, and the unwavering spirit of partnership in fulfilling a divine purpose. Their adventure served as an inspiring reminder that every individual matters, that guidance is a treasured gift, and that together, they could illuminate the path for countless others seeking God's will for their lives.

THE BENEFITS AND CHALLENGES OF THE TIMOTHY AND PAUL PARTNERSHIP

In the sacred alliance between Timothy and Paul lies a profound lesson in the beauty of mentorship—where guidance becomes a source of strength, inspiration, and growth. This partnership exemplifies how shared faith can illuminate the path forward for both mentor and mentee, forging connections that echo through time. The benefits are multifaceted:

1. Through steadfast support, Timothy found his voice and purpose and became the Pastor of the powerful New Testament Church of Ephesus.
2. The Apostle Paul found his next assignment in nurturing the next generation. This passion reinforced his legacy and renewed his own spirit.

Their relationship serves as a reminder that when we unite in purpose, we amplify our collective impact, cultivating a community bound by love and mutual respect.

However, navigating this dynamic partnership is not without its challenges. Differences in experience, perspective, and approach can create friction if not addressed with care and compassion. Timothy, eager and youthful, may occasionally struggle under the weight of his mentor's towering expectations, while Paul, entrenched in his wisdom, might find it difficult to step back and allow

Timothy the space to grow in his own right. To foster growth within this relationship, both must practice open communication, embracing vulnerability as a pathway to understanding.

"Challenges are not obstacles but opportunities for deeper connection." - Jonathan Vorce

By recognizing this truth we can learn to lean on each other, transforming our trials into stepping stones toward greater empathy, resilience, and success.

In our modern landscape, we can look to this strategic partnership as an inspiring blueprint for our own relationships—whether in faith communities, workplaces, or personal lives. To navigate the complexities inherent in mentorship, we should prioritize active listening and intentional dialogue, allowing all voices to be heard and valued. It is through this nurturing of individuality within the collective that we come to experience true growth. By celebrating each other's achievements and offering compassion during moments of struggle, we strengthen our bonds and create a flourishing environment for all. Let us embrace the spirit of Timothy and Paul, confident that through collaboration, understanding, and faith, we can chart a course toward a more hopeful and united future, illuminating the way for ourselves and those who follow.

REFLECTIONS ON THE STRATEGIC PARTNERSHIP: LESSONS OF GROWTH, UNITY, AND DIVINE WISDOM

It has been said that we are not called to compete with one another but to complete each other. The partnership between Timothy and Paul serves as a sacred testament to the power of mentorship and the divine exchange of wisdom that interweaves through generations. From their journey, we draw profound insights that resonate deeply with our own spiritual quests. One significant lesson is the transformative nature of vulnerability; it is in the openness of sharing struggles and triumphs that genuine connection flourishes. Timothy's willingness to lean on Paul for guidance, paired with Paul's patience and nurturing spirit, illustrates that growth is not a solitary endeavor but a shared journey that enhances our collective strength.

The transformative nature of vulnerability invites us to acknowledge our imperfections and fears, offering them as gifts in the realm of human connection. In the dynamic between Timothy and Paul, we witness how their shared experiences forged an unbreakable bond, one that exuded grace and understanding. Timothy's courage to voice his challenges stemmed not only from a trust in Paul's wisdom but from a deep-seated belief that through sharing his heart, he would find solace and guidance. Meanwhile, Paul's nurturing spirit provided a safe haven for Timothy to explore his doubts, reinforcing the notion that mentorship flourishes when both parties embrace the beauty of vulnerability.

This sacred exchange between mentor and mentee fosters an environment where growth thrives. As they navigate their journey together, they learn to celebrate not just victories but also lessons gleaned from missteps and uncertainties. Each struggle shared weaves a tapestry of experiences that enriches their relationship, allowing them to conquer trials as allies rather than individuals. In this way, vulnerability becomes a bridge connecting hearts, revealing that we are not alone in our pursuits and challenges. By opening ourselves to one another, we create a bedrock of support that nurtures our collective strength, empowering each of us to rise higher together.

The challenges faced in the partnership between Timothy and Paul remind us that each obstacle is imbued with purpose. Every trial presents an opportunity to deepen their understanding of one another and the difficulties they encounter. This shared understanding significantly strengthens their resilience and unity. The privilege of learning and growing together fosters a wealth of Godly wisdom, enabling both mentor and mentee to become greater vessels of compassion and insight.

Through their shared purpose and divine guidance, we witness the profound power of mentorship, illuminating a path of hope and inspiration for future generations. Ultimately, the partnership between Timothy and Paul exemplifies the transformative nature of vulnerability, the beauty of collaboration, and the guiding influence of faith in shaping our journeys toward growth and unity. Let us embrace these lessons with open hearts, recognizing that together we can achieve greatness beyond measure.

TIMOTHY AND PAUL - A SPIRITUAL BOND

The relationship between Timothy and Paul exemplifies one of the most profound examples of mentorship in the Bible. It highlights the deep connections that can be forged when faith and guidance take center stage. Paul, an apostle who faced numerous trials and tribulations for his unwavering faith in Christ, took Timothy under his wing when he recognized the young man's potential and dedication. In 2 Timothy 1:5, Paul fondly recalls Timothy's sincere faith, which first lived in his grandmother Lois and his mother Eunice, and now flourishes within Timothy himself. This generational passing of faith underscores the vital role that family and community play in nurturing spiritual growth, emphasizing how beliefs and values are often cultivated in the home before being carried into the wider world.

Paul's influence in Timothy's life transcended the traditional role of a teacher; he became a spiritual father figure to the young man. Through their relationship, Paul provided not only education but also emotional and spiritual support, guiding Timothy through various journeys and challenges he faced in his ministry. Paul's letters to Timothy are treasures filled with wisdom, encouragement, and specific instructions aimed at fortifying Timothy's faith and enhancing his leadership abilities.

In addition to teaching him doctrine, Paul shared personal experiences that shaped his own faith, offering Timothy insights into the realities of being a leader in the early church. He encouraged Timothy to embrace his unique calling and to not be afraid to stand firm in his beliefs, even in the face of adversity. This mentorship was marked by a deep bond forged through prayer, shared experiences, and mutual respect, illustrating how meaningful relationships can empower individuals to grow spiritually and fulfill their destinies. Ultimately, the mentorship dynamic between Paul and Timothy serves as a powerful reminder of the impact one person can have on another's spiritual journey, reinforcing the importance of guiding the next generation in their pursuit of faith.

ELEMENTS OF PAUL'S MENTORSHIP

Paul's mentorship of Timothy was rooted in a deep sense of compassion and understanding. He recognized the struggles and challenges that Timothy faced as a young leader, and he patiently guided him through each obstacle with love and grace. Furthermore, Paul's approach to mentoring reflected the transformative nature of vulnerability, creating an environment where Timothy felt safe to share his doubts and fears without judgment. The following are just three of the elements that Paul taught Pastor Timothy.

Faith

Paul's primary focus was on nurturing Timothy's faith, emphasizing its importance in his spiritual journey. He reminded Timothy of the deep-rooted faith that he had inherited from his grandmother and mother, highlighting the legacy of belief that had been passed down through generations. Paul encouraged him to fan into flame the gift of God, which signifies not only the initial spark of faith but also the ongoing commitment to develop it further. This call to rekindle faith serves as a powerful reminder of the continuous need to nurture and grow one's spiritual life, fostering resilience and strength in the face of challenges and deepening one's connection to God.

Character

"Your talents may take you to the top, but it takes good character and integrity to keep you there." - Jonathan Vorce.

This statement serves as a reminder that while skills and abilities can propel us to success, it is our moral compass and ethical foundation that will sustain that success over time.

The Apostle Paul, in his letters, underscored the crucial role of character in leadership by mentoring Timothy. He urged Timothy to actively pursue qualities such as righteousness, godliness, faith, love, endurance, and gentleness. These virtues are not just desirable traits; they are essential for any leader aspiring to make a lasting impact. Developing such qualities requires dedication and commitment, often best achieved through consistent mentorship, supportive relationships, and personal discipline. By cultivating these attributes, individuals not only enhance their own leadership capabilities but also inspire those around them, creating a positive ripple effect in their communities and beyond.

Leadership

"Everything rises and falls on leadership." - John C. Maxwell

In his letters, Paul meticulously prepared Timothy for effective leadership by offering practical and actionable advice tailored for leading a church community. He emphasized the importance of addressing critical issues such as dealing with false teachers who may undermine the faith of others, maintaining sound doctrine to ensure that the teachings align with the core beliefs of Christianity, and setting a good example for others to follow through his own behavior and actions.

Leadership, particularly in the Christian context, transcends mere authority; it is fundamentally about serving others with humility and grace. It involves being a living testament to Christ-like behavior, embodying love, compassion, and integrity in every interaction. This model of leadership encourages the growth and development of others in the faith, fostering a supportive environment where individuals can thrive spiritually and contribute positively to their community. By nurturing these qualities, a leader not only strengthens their own faith but also inspires and uplifts those around them.

PRACTICAL APPLICATIONS FOR MODERN CHRISTIAN LEADERS

As we reflect on the profound mentorship that Paul provided to Timothy, modern Christian leaders can draw from these timeless principles to navigate the complexities of today's spiritual landscape. The essence of Paul's teachings offers a roadmap rooted in faith, character, and leadership—each element ripe with practical applications that can empower and inspire this generation of leaders.

Cultivating a Strong Faith Foundation

In a world filled with distractions and uncertainties, it is vital for leaders to cultivate a deep and resilient faith. This involves not only personal study and prayer but also creating spaces for communal worship and fellowship. Modern leaders can adopt practices such as regular Bible study groups, spiritual retreats, and mentorship circles, where they can share their journeys and reinforce each other's beliefs. By actively engaging in these communal experiences, leaders foster an environment that encourages spiritual growth and provides the support necessary to confront personal and communal challenges with unwavering faith.

Embodying Christ-like Character

Leaders today must prioritize the development of character as a cornerstone of their influence. This entails living out virtues such as integrity, humility, and compassion in their daily lives. Practical applications include establishing accountability partnerships, participating in service-oriented projects, and seeking feedback from trusted mentors or peers. Emphasizing transparency in actions helps leaders resonate with their communities, demonstrating that true leadership is about service rather than authority. By embodying these characteristics, leaders not only enhance their credibility but also inspire those around them to pursue similar virtues in their lives.

Engaging in Servant Leadership

The model of leadership established by Paul emphasizes servanthood as the essence of effective leadership—an approach that is highly relevant today. Modern Christian leaders should strive to be accessible and supportive, empowering others toward their own paths of faith. This can be achieved through mentorship programs, community outreach initiatives, and genuine listening to the concerns and needs of their congregations. By prioritizing the well-being and growth of others, leaders create a culture of encouragement and unity, reminding their communities that they are all on this spiritual journey together.

Addressing Contemporary Challenges with Wisdom

Just as Paul guided Timothy in confronting false teachings and ensuring sound doctrine, modern leaders must be vigilant and informed. This means staying aware of the cultural and theological challenges facing today's church, including the rise of secularism, social justice issues, and the intersection of faith and modern technology. Engaging in continuous learning through theological education, workshops, and conferences enables leaders to equip themselves with the knowledge necessary to guide their communities in truth. Furthermore, fostering a collective discernment process—encouraging dialogue and debate rooted in scripture—can empower communities to respond collaboratively to contemporary issues while remaining anchored in their faith.

In summary, by applying the principles exemplified in Paul's mentorship of Timothy, contemporary Christian leaders can cultivate a faith-driven environment that nurtures character and embodies Christ-like service. Through intentional practices, they can navigate the complexities of leadership with compassion and wisdom, inviting their communities to thrive spiritually amid the challenges of our time.

THE ENDURING IMPACT OF MENTORING IN FAITH COMMUNITIES

The relationship between Timothy and Paul serves as a poignant illustration of the transformative power of mentorship within faith communities. Their bond transcended a mere teacher-student dynamic; instead, it blossomed into a profound legacy that would resonate through generations of believers. This mentorship highlights several critical components that contribute to individual growth and community resilience—elements that modern Christian leaders can adopt to foster spiritual flourishing in their congregations.

At its core, **mentorship is a conduit for spiritual discipleship**. Paul's investment in Timothy was not only a means of imparting knowledge but also a profound exercise in sharing life experiences, prayer, and mutual encouragement. Through their interactions, Timothy gained valuable insights into the Christian faith and deftly learned how to navigate the complexities of leadership. This formative influence fortified Timothy's faith, providing him with the tools to confront challenges while remaining anchored in truth. In today's contexts, such mentoring relationships are invaluable; they establish networks of support that encourage openness and accountability, allowing individuals to explore their faith journeys within a safe and nurturing environment.

Moreover, **mentoring cultivates community cohesion**. As Timothy found strength and guidance through Paul's mentorship, the church community thrived under the shared values and teachings that emerged from their relationship. Modern Christian leaders can create similar dynamics by prioritizing mentoring as a foundational aspect of their ministry. Initiating mentorship programs that connect seasoned believers with newcomers or young leaders can foster a sense of belonging. These relationships encourage the sharing of wisdom, testimonies, and faith experiences, which fortifies the community's collective identity and reinforces its purpose. In this manner, mentoring becomes a vital thread that unites congregants, cultivating a vibrant atmosphere where individuals are uplifted and empowered to contribute positively to their spiritual family.

The impact of **mentoring** extends beyond individual growth and community building; it **sets the stage for generational continuity within faith communities**. Paul's encouragement to Timothy was not limited to immediate concerns; rather, it laid the groundwork for future leaders in the church. By nurturing Timothy's growth, Paul ensured that the essence of their teachings would be perpetuated, allowing the faith to thrive long after their time together. This legacy reflects a broader truth: when leaders invest in the development of others, they plant seeds of faith that can yield an abundant harvest for future generations. For contemporary leaders, embracing this legacy means making mentorship an intentional practice, encouraging seasoned members to take active roles in guiding newer believers. Such actions ensure that the values, teachings, and goals of the community are preserved and passed down, allowing faith to flourish over time.

In conclusion, the enduring impact of mentorship—as exemplified by Paul and Timothy—reveals the depth of connection that can be fostered within faith communities. By embracing and implementing effective mentoring practices, modern Christian leaders can nurture individual faith, build resilient communities, and cultivate the next generation of believers. This compassionate and intentional approach to mentorship not only echoes the teachings of scripture but also embodies the heart of Christ's mission: to love, empower, and uplift one another on our shared spiritual journey.

JESUS AND HIS DISCIPLES

FELLOWSHIP, DISCIPLESHIP, MISSION

Matthew 28:19-20

In the sun-drenched hills of Galilee, where the azure sky kissed the golden earth, a gathering of souls formed a vibrant tapestry of fellowship and faith. The air was alive with the fragrance of olive trees, the laughter of children echoed from nearby villages, and fishermen's boats bobbed gently upon the tranquil waters. Here, amidst the simplicity and beauty of creation, Jesus walked among His disciples, His words flowing like the sweetest melody, beckoning hearts to awaken to a mission far greater than themselves.

The disciples, a diverse band of ordinary men, were drawn to Him—each called from their daily toils, each with a story woven with struggles, doubts, and dreams. As they sat on sun-warmed stones, surrounded by lush green pastures and the distant sound of rushing streams, Jesus shared visions of a Kingdom filled with love and compassion. He painted a picture of a world where hearts connected through mercy and hope, illustrating the power of their unity as a strategic partnership to spread His word to the ends of the earth. In those moments, He ignited a spark in their souls—a collective flame of purpose burning bright against the shadows of fear and uncertainty.

The days turned into weeks as they journeyed together, their feet trudging along dusty paths, their voices harmonizing in prayer and song. As they healed the sick, fed the hungry, and welcomed the outcast, a divine energy surged through their fellowship, binding them in a mission of love. Every healing miracle was a reminder of their purpose; each whispered parable held the weight of change. The laughter shared around evening fires resonated with hope, affirming that no heart was meant to journey alone.

As this profound mission unfurled, the ripple effects began to resonate throughout the land. The parables conveyed by fishermen and tax collectors transcended barriers, spreading beyond a village's borders like wildflower seeds carried by the wind. Jesus' call for discipleship morphed into a movement—a vibrant culture rooted in love, serving as a beacon of light amid the daily struggles of life. This strategic partnership, forged in faith, discipleship, and fellowship, embedded itself in the hearts of those who heard, seen in their willingness to respond to the call, to live out their faith boldly and compassionately.

Today, the essence of that fellowship still thrives

among us. Across cities and nations, in communities large and small, we continue to respond to that ancient call. We gather in circles of love, just as those first disciples did, sharing our testimonies of grace and hope, echoing the mission of our savior in new and innovative ways. The Spirit of Jesus weaves through the fabric of our lives, inspiring strategic partnerships that reach out to the lonely, uplift the downtrodden, and light the path toward unity and understanding. Each act of kindness, each moment of compassion, is a testament that the fellowship birthed on the shores of Galilee is not just history but a living, breathing call to action that pulses through our very being. In this way, the legacy of Jesus and His disciples continues to unfold, inviting us all to be part of a divine story that transcends time and space.

EMBRACING THE BENEFITS AND NAVIGATING THE CHALLENGES OF THIS STRATEGIC PARTNERSHIP

In the light of Jesus' teachings and the profound fellowship of His disciples, we find both inspirational benefits and significant challenges that resonate with our present context. The first and most evident benefit is the power of unity. When we align our hearts and minds in a strategic partnership, we cultivate a sense of belonging and purpose, fostering an environment where love thrives. This shared mission allows us to pool our resources, diverse talents, and unique perspectives, creating a unique oasis of strength that empowers us to effect meaningful change in our communities. Whether it is through collaborative outreach initiatives, community service projects, or support networks, the synergy that arises transforms ambitions into actions that serve the greater good and demonstrate God's love in our modern world.

Yet, with great potential comes great intricacies. Challenges such as differing visions, communication barriers, and potential conflicts can arise, threatening to fracture the very unity we work to maintain. In our contemporary era, where individualism often prevails, the call to collective action may feel daunting. However, it is in facing these challenges that we are given the opportunity for growth. By approaching conflicts with compassion, embracing open dialogue, and seeking understanding over agreement, we can nurture resilience within our partnerships. It is essential to remind ourselves that the strength of a strategic partnership lies in unity, not in uniformity, as we celebrate our differences as gifts that contribute to a more profound purpose.

As we learn to harness the benefits and navigate the challenges of our strategic partnerships, we align ourselves more closely with the transformative mission of Jesus and His disciples. Together, we embark on a journey of shared purpose, allowing our collective light to shine brightly in the world, dispelling darkness and fostering hope in every heart we touch. In this sacred collaboration, we not only seek mutual success but also embrace the divine potential within each of us, awakening the spirit of community that mirrors the beloved fellowship that began in Galilee.

UNDERSTANDING THE SIGNIFICANCE OF FELLOWSHIP IN CHRISTIAN COMMUNITY

Fellowship stands as a cornerstone of the Christian faith, transcending mere gatherings to forge a deep spiritual connection that embodies the love of Christ. In the early church, believers showed their commitment to this fellowship by immersing themselves in the teachings of the Apostles, sharing meals, singing, worshiping, and engaging in prayer together. This communal bond provided essential strength and encouragement, enabling them to spread the Gospel even in the face of persecution, as highlighted in Acts 2:42-47, where it is written,

> *"They devoted themselves to the apostles' teaching and to fellowship, to the breaking of bread and to prayer."*

In our contemporary world, the essence of fellowship continues to be indispensable. It creates a nurturing atmosphere where believers can cultivate their spiritual lives, offer one another support, and collaborate in the pursuit of fulfilling the Great Commission, as instructed in Matthew 28:19-20. Within this community, individuals encourage one another through shared experiences and wisdom, becoming a living testament to Christ's teachings. The collective efforts of a unified body in faith amplify the impact of their mission, reminding us that we are stronger together.

Ultimately, fellowship is not merely a social activity; it is a divine calling—a sacred opportunity to reflect Christ's love in our relationships and to grow together in faith. As we carve out time for one another, we embrace the beauty of community and allow our collective spirit to shine brightly in a world longing for connection and hope.

UNDERSTANDING THE SIGNIFICANCE OF DISCIPLESHIP IN CHRISTIAN COMMUNITY

Discipleship is essential to the Christian faith, serving as the bridge that connects personal belief to collective action. It is the process through which individuals not only learn about Jesus Christ but also grow in their relationship with Him and each other. In the Great Commission, Jesus commanded His followers, saying,

> "Go therefore and make disciples of all nations" - Matthew 28:19 ESV.

This calling is not just about teaching but embodies a lifestyle of learning, growing, and imitating Christ.

In the early church, discipleship was demonstrated through immersive experiences, prayer, and communal gatherings, fostering a strong sense of commitment among believers. This engagement nurtured an environment ripe for spiritual growth, as seen in Acts 2:46, where it is written,

> "And day by day, attending the temple together and breaking bread in their homes, they received their food with glad and generous hearts."

Such unity in mission and purpose enabled them to withstand trials and share the message of love and hope, even amidst adversity.

Today, the importance of discipleship remains vital as it creates a framework for believers to support one another in their spiritual journeys. When Christians commit to walking alongside each other, they cultivate a community of accountability, encouragement, and shared wisdom. This collective effort propels individuals towards their God-given potential, allowing the light of Christ to shine through their actions and interactions. As we strive to fulfill the essence of discipleship, we echo the words of Hebrews 10:24-25, which remind us to

"consider how to stir up one another to love and good works, not neglecting to meet together, as is the habit of some, but encouraging one another."

Ultimately, discipleship within a Christian community is a transformative journey. It invites each of us to step out of solitude into a holy fellowship characterized by mutual growth and nurturing relationships. As we live out our roles as disciples, we contribute to a vibrant, dynamic community that embodies Christ's love and mission, demonstrating that we are, indeed, stronger when we walk together in faith.

UNDERSTANDING THE SIGNIFICANCE OF JESUS' MISSION IN THE CHRISTIAN COMMUNITY

The mission of Jesus was straightforward and unwavering: to seek and save those who are lost. As it is written in Luke 19:10,

> *"For the Son of Man came to seek and to save the lost."*

Jesus' ministry was filled with acts of compassion, healing, teaching, and, ultimately, sacrifice. His life serves as a blueprint for how we, as modern Christians, should live.

For us today, this mission carries on. We are called to be the hands and feet of Jesus, extending love and assistance to those in need, sharing the message of salvation, and embodying the values of the Kingdom of God. This calling isn't limited to the confines of our church buildings but extends far beyond—to our workplaces, neighborhoods, and even to strangers we meet in our daily lives.

Imagine living each day with the intention of reflecting Christ's love and mercy. By doing so, we can profoundly impact the lives of those around us, drawing others closer to Him. Whether it's through simple acts of kindness, offering a listening ear, or providing support to someone going through a tough time, we have countless opportunities to live out Jesus' mission every day.

Jesus' ministry teaches us the power of compassion

and sacrifice. He healed the sick, comforted the brokenhearted, and taught with wisdom and love. We, too, are invited to bring healing to our communities. This might mean volunteering at local shelters, mentoring youth, or simply being present for those who need us.

By living out these principles, we not only honor Jesus' mission but also experience a deeper connection to our faith and to each other. In doing so, we become beacons of hope and love in a world that desperately needs both.

JESUS' TEACHINGS ON COMPASSION AND HOW WE CAN LIVE THEM TODAY

Jesus' teachings on compassion are among the most profound and enduring aspects of His ministry. Through His words and actions, He showed us that compassion is a cornerstone of a life lived in love and service to others.

One of the most powerful illustrations of Jesus' message on compassion is the Parable of the Good Samaritan (Luke 10:25-37). In this story, a man is beaten, robbed, and left for dead on the side of the road. Several people pass by without offering help. However, a Samaritan—a person from a group often despised by the Jews at the time—stops to care for the injured man. He tends to his wounds, takes him to an inn, and ensures he receives the care he needs. Jesus used this parable to teach that our neighbor is anyone in need, and true compassion knows no boundaries of race, religion, or social status.

Another key teaching on compassion comes from the Sermon on the Mount (Matthew 5-7). In this sermon,

Jesus outlines the attitudes and actions that reflect the heart of God. He speaks of mercy, peacemaking, and loving our enemies. Jesus tells us to

> "do unto others as you would have them do unto you" - Matthew 7:12,

often referred to as the Golden Rule. This teaching encourages us to treat others with the same kindness and empathy we desire for ourselves.

These teachings are not just lofty ideals; they offer practical guidance for our everyday lives. Imagine a world where we all strive to live out the compassion Jesus preached. Here are some ways we can bring His teachings into our daily routines:

1. **Acts of Kindness**: Small gestures can make a big difference. Holding the door for someone, offering a smile, or helping a neighbor with their groceries are simple ways to show compassion.
2. **Empathy and Listening**: Taking the time to listen to others and understand their struggles can be incredibly healing. Whether it's a friend going through a tough time or a co-worker who needs a listening ear, your presence can provide comfort and support.
3. **Volunteering**: Give your time to causes that help those in need. Volunteering at a food bank, mentoring youth, or participating in

community clean-up efforts are all ways to extend compassion in tangible ways.
4. **Support in Times of Crisis**: When someone is facing a crisis, whether it's illness, loss, or financial hardship, offering support can be life-changing. This might mean providing meals, helping with errands, or simply being there to offer emotional support.

By embodying these principles, we follow in Jesus' footsteps, becoming vessels of His love and compassion in the world. As we practice kindness and empathy, we not only bring healing to others but also experience a deeper connection to our faith and to each other. In living out Jesus' teachings on compassion, we become beacons of hope and love, reflecting the divine light that's within us all.

A CLOSER LOOK AT THE GREAT COMMISSION

Matthew 28:19-20, widely recognized as the Great Commission, serves as a pivotal scripture for all believers. In this scripture, Jesus commands,

> *"Go therefore and make disciples of all nations, baptizing them in the name of the Father, and of the Son, and of the Holy Spirit, teaching them to observe all things that I have commanded you; and lo, I am with you always, even to the end of the age."*

This powerful directive encompasses several key elements that provide insight into the mission entrusted to His followers:

1. **Go** – This word signifies more than just movement; it embodies a call to action and intentionality. Believers are encouraged to actively seek out opportunities to share their faith, whether through personal relationships, community involvement, or global missions. It emphasizes the necessity of stepping out of comfort zones to reach others.
2. **Make Disciples** – The emphasis here is not merely on converting individuals but on fostering a deeper relationship with Christ. This involves nurturing new believers into mature followers who will grow in their faith and, in turn, multiply by sharing the Gospel with others. Discipleship is a lifelong journey of learning and transformation.
3. **Baptize** – Baptism symbolizes an act of initiation and identification with the Christian faith. It serves as an outward expression of an inward change, marking the beginning of a believer's journey with Christ. This sacrament unites individuals with the global community of believers and signifies their commitment to following Him.
4. **Teach** – Ongoing instruction in the ways of Christ is essential for spiritual growth. This

encompasses not just theological knowledge but also practical application of biblical principles in everyday life. Teaching encourages believers to live out their faith authentically and to help others understand the teachings of Jesus.

The Great Commission is both a privilege and responsibility for every believer. It serves as a guiding principle, reminding us that we are called to spread the Gospel with urgency and dedication. Embracing this mission requires commitment, courage, and a willingness to engage with the world around us, knowing that we are not alone in this endeavor—Jesus promises to be with us always, even to the end of the age. As we fulfill this commission, we contribute to the fulfillment of God's purpose on earth.

CONCLUSION - ENCOURAGEMENT TO EMBRACE FELLOWSHIP, DISCIPLESHIP, AND MISSION IN DAILY LIFE

In the serene landscapes of Galilee, where the delicate morning mists kissed the earth, Jesus embarked on a journey with His disciples that would forever alter the course of humanity. Their strategic partnership, rooted in fellowship, discipleship, and mission, offers timeless insights and experiences that continue to nurture our spiritual growth and unity today.

Fellowship with Jesus was not merely about gathering; it was a sacred communion, a coming together of hearts in love and hope. As His disciples listened to His teachings, shared meals, and prayed together, they surrendered to a unity that transcended their individual struggles and doubts. This fellowship became their strength, a divine energy that surged through their collective mission to heal, uplift, and spread the Gospel. Likewise, our modern communities find strength in fellowship, where every shared moment becomes a thread in the fabric of divine connection, fostering a sense of belonging and purpose.

Discipleship, as demonstrated by Jesus and His followers, was a transformative journey. It was a call to leave behind the familiar and step into the unknown with faith. The disciples learned not just through words but through lived experiences—walking side by side with Jesus, witnessing miracles, and embracing the divine teachings that reshaped their lives. Today, discipleship remains a vital aspect of our spiritual journey, urging us to grow in our relationship with Christ and each other. By committing to discipleship, we cultivate a community of accountability and support, encouraging one another to reflect Christ's love in our actions.

The mission of Jesus, to seek and save the lost, was imbued with compassion and unwavering dedication. His strategic partnership with the disciples was a testament to the power of collective effort in fulfilling a divine purpose. As they ventured into villages and towns, healing the sick and welcoming the outcast, they embodied the essence of His mission—transforming lives through love and mercy. In our contemporary world, this mission continues to inspire us, guiding our endeavors to reach out to those in need, uplift the downtrodden, and spread hope and kindness.

Reflecting on these profound lessons, we see how the strategic partnership of Jesus and His disciples offers a blueprint for our spiritual journey. It teaches us the value of fellowship, the transformative power of discipleship, and the enduring impact of a mission rooted in love. As we navigate the challenges of our modern context, these principles foster growth, unity, and divine wisdom, illuminating our path and reinforcing our bond as a faith community.

In every act of kindness, every shared prayer, and every moment of compassion, we echo the legacy of Jesus and His disciples. Their journey from the hills of Galilee to the ends of the earth continues to resonate within us, inviting us to partake in a divine story that transcends time. Together, we embrace this sacred collaboration, allowing the spirit of fellowship, discipleship, and mission to guide us toward a future filled with hope, unity, and boundless love.

JESUS AND HIS CHURCH TODAY

CONTINUING THE MISSION THROUGH THE GREAT COMMISSION

𝓜atthew 28:19-20
As the radiant dawn of a new day broke, the first light gently embraced the hills and cityscape, illuminating the vibrant heart of a diverse and bustling community. Jesus, the embodiment of compassion and wisdom, stands at the center, extending an invitation to all who would listen. His voice, warm like the sun breaking through a cool mist, fills souls with inspiration and purpose. Imagine, for a moment, the sights of dusty streets where children laugh and play, their joyous echoes mingling with the whispers of the faithful—a community yearning for hope, just as they did in years gone by.

Like the vibrant hues of a sunset that paints the heavens, Jesus calls forth His Church—an assembly not defined by walls, but by the unity and spirit of its members. Each believer becomes a brushstroke in this divine masterpiece, collaborating in a strategic partnership that transcends time. The sacred texts flutter like autumn leaves, their messages alive with passion and energy, encouraging the faithful to arise and embark on a journey of love, healing, and transformation.

Consider the camaraderie between believers, reminiscent of early disciples who, hand in hand, faced adversity with unwavering faith. Together, they become the living embodiment of the Great Commission, harnessing the power of the Holy Spirit to spread the revolutionary message of grace. Picture them, amidst the everyday hustle, sharing heartwarming stories of hope over shared meals, their laughter punctuating the air like joyous bells ringing on a festive day. Each interaction—a sacred weaving of lives connecting through purpose, ignited for the common good.

As they gather in humble homes and open fields, their hearts ablaze with devotion, they reimagine community. The spirit of Jesus flows through them like a gentle breeze, igniting flames of creativity and compassion that leap beyond societal norms, inviting those around them to embrace grace and healing. The vibrant tapestry of faith glimmers, showcasing a world transformed, one soul at a time, making the message of Calvary resonate as fervently as it did two millennia ago. In this strategic partnership, the Church of today is not merely a vessel; it is a powerful lighthouse, shining brightly against the currents of despair, ever beckoning to the weary and seeking hearts to come home.

Pastor, Preacher, Theologian, and Christian Apologist, Timothy Keller, reminds us,

"Jesus didn't just come to show us how to live; He came to change our very hearts and give us a mission that transcends time." *

What does it mean to fulfill the mission of Jesus in today's world? It's a question that resonates deeply within the Christian community, church leaders, and theologians alike. The Great Commission, found in Matthew 28:19-20, is not just a historical mandate but a living command that continues to shape the mission and vision of the Church today.

In this chapter, we'll explore the significance of the Great Commission, its historical and cultural context, theological insights, contemporary examples, and practical strategies for modern believers and churches to continue Jesus' mission in the modern world. Whether you're a seasoned theologian or a passionate church leader, this discussion will provide valuable insights and inspiration for engaging in mission work today.

UNDERSTANDING THE GREAT COMMISSION

The Great Commission is one of the most pivotal

---

* **Footnote:** Timothy Keller *"The Reason for God"* (Penguin Books, August 4, 2009).

commands given by Jesus to His disciples. Found in Matthew 28:19-20, it reads:

> *"Therefore go and make disciples of all nations, baptizing them in the name of the Father and of the Son and of the Holy Spirit, and teaching them to obey everything I have commanded you. And surely I am with you always, to the very end of the age."*

This command was not only directed at the disciples present at that moment in history but also extends to all believers throughout the ages, reaching across generations and cultures. It encapsulates the very essence of the Christian mission: to spread the Gospel, which is the good news of Jesus Christ, disciple others by nurturing their faith, and teach them to live according to the profound teachings and example set by Jesus. This call to action encourages every believer to actively participate in a transformative journey, fostering a community rooted in love, service, and the teachings of Christ, thereby ensuring that the message of hope continues to resonate in the hearts of many.

Historical and Cultural Context of Matthew 28:19-20

To fully appreciate the significance of the Great Commission, we need to look at its historical and cultural context. Jesus gave this command after His resurrection, during a time when His disciples were still coming to terms with His departure from this world. He spoke these words in Galilee, a region known for its diverse population and rich cultural interactions.

When Jesus said, *"make disciples of all nations,"* it was a groundbreaking directive. This command was not just a simple instruction; it was a call to break down existing barriers within Judaism and to adopt a more worldwide approach to spreading the Gospel. This inclusivity marked a radical departure from the religious norms of that time, emphasizing that the message of Christ was meant for everyone, regardless of their background.

By commanding His disciples to reach out to all nations, Jesus was essentially ushering in a new era of understanding and acceptance. He was reinforcing the idea that God's love and salvation were available to all humanity, resonating with the scripture in Galatians 3:28,

> *"There is neither Jew nor Gentile, neither slave nor free, nor is there male and female, for you are all one in Christ Jesus."*

This powerful message resonates deeply, reminding us that faith transcends all cultural and social boundaries. At its core, this passage challenges the societal norms and divisions that were prevalent in Paul's time—and continues to resonate with the issues of division and inequality today.

In exploring this verse more deeply, it's essential to understand the context in which Paul wrote these words. The early Christian community was grappling with how Jewish and Gentile believers could coexist. There were debates over whether Gentile converts needed to adhere to Jewish customs. In addressing these concerns, Paul emphasizes that faith in Christ Jesus abolishes all divisions created by social status, ethnicity, or gender.

The phrase *"neither Jew nor Gentile"* underscores the elimination of ethnic barriers. Through faith in Christ, all are invited into God's covenant family without distinction—a revolutionary concept at a time when ethnic identity deeply influenced religious practice and social interactions.

Furthermore, Paul also highlights the equality of genders in the community of believers. In a society where women were often seen as inferior and had limited rights, Paul's proclamation that *"there is neither male nor female"* carries significant significance. It challenges the traditional hierarchical structures and affirms women's invaluable standing in the eyes of God.

Ultimately, Paul's message emphasizes the unifying power of faith in Christ. No longer bound by societal norms or cultural divisions, believers are brought together as one body through their shared identity as followers of Jesus. This unity extends beyond social status or ethnic background and creates a new community founded on grace, acceptance, and mutual respect.

In our modern world where division and discrimination still exist, Paul's words serve as a powerful reminder of the transformative and inclusive nature of Christianity. It calls for believers to continue breaking down barriers and striving towards unity, mirroring the example set by Jesus himself. By embracing Paul's message, we can create a more just and equitable society where all are treated with dignity and respect.

Furthermore, Paul's teachings on gender equality also have relevance in today's discussions on women's roles in leadership within the church. His recognition of women as invaluable and useful members in the body of Christ challenges the ancient structures that have historically marginalized their voices. As we seek to build an inclusive church community, Paul's words remind us to value and empower both men and women in their service to God.

Therefore, Paul's proclamation of *"neither male nor female"* carries profound implications for our understanding of each individuals holy mandate , and unity within the church. His message serves as a call to action, challenging us to actively work towards a community where all are valued and treated with respect. As we continue to learn from Paul's words, may we strive towards building a more united and just society within the body of Christ, reflecting the example set by Jesus himself.

THEOLOGICAL INSIGHTS INTO THE NATURE OF THE CHURCH

The Great Commission serves as a profound testament to the true nature of the Church, revealing it not merely as a static assembly of believers but as a vibrant, missional community. This commission, given by Christ Himself, calls the Church to transcend its walls and engage actively with the world, sharing the transformative message of Christ's love and redemption.

At the heart of this mission-driven identity is the very nature of God, who, in His infinite love and grace, seeks to reconcile all of creation to Himself. This divine purpose is not a supplementary aspect of the Church's existence; rather, it is the essence of the Church's being. Theologian N. T. Wright poignantly captures this truth by stating,

> *"The Church exists for mission in the same way that fire exists for burning."* *

Mission work, therefore, is not an optional activity or a peripheral program but the core of what it means to be the Church.

Understanding the Church as a missional community fundamentally shapes how believers perceive their role in the world. It invites each member to participate in God's redemptive plan actively, fostering a collective sense of purpose and direction. This mission-driven ethos propels the Church to engage with society compassionately and intentionally, serving as a beacon of hope and a vessel of God's love.

Moreover, this perspective emphasizes that the Church's mission is deeply intertwined with the character of God. Just as God is relentlessly committed to restoring

---

* **Footnote:** N. T. Wright, *Simply Jesus: A New Vision of Who He Was, What He Did, and Why He Matters* (HarperOne, 2011).

and healing creation, so too is the Church called to mirror this divine initiative. This alignment with God's nature infuses the Church's mission with a deep sense of reverence and responsibility.

The implications for believers are deeply significant. Recognizing the Church's mission-driven identity means acknowledging that every act of kindness, every effort to spread the gospel, and every initiative to serve the community is a reflection of God's ongoing work in the world. It is through these actions that the Church fulfills its divine mandate, becoming a living testament to God's reconciling love.

In embracing this understanding, the Church must continuously seek ways to embody this missional calling in its daily life. Whether through local outreach programs, global missions, or personal acts of service, the Church is called to be an active participant in God's redemptive story. This journey of engagement not only transforms communities but also draws believers closer to the heart of God, fostering a deep, abiding sense of connection and divine protection.

In essence, the nature of the Church as a missional community is a beautiful reflection of God's unwavering commitment to creation. It is a call to live out the Great Commission with sincerity and devotion, ensuring that the Church remains a dynamic force for good, continually pointing the world to the boundless love and grace of God.

Case Study
Grace Community Church's Mission Work

In the heart of a bustling metropolis, where skyscrapers traversed the clouds and diverse cultures intertwined, stood Grace Community Church—a place not merely defined by its brick and mortar but by the warmth of love, acceptance, and a fervent desire to serve. The church's vibrant community was inspired by the teachings of Christ, embodying the mission-led ethos that their faith called upon them to live out.

One fateful spring, as the flowers began to bloom and spirits were lifted with the promise of renewal, a group of members from Grace Community Church felt a divine whisper—a calling to extend their arms beyond their sanctuary's walls. Recognizing the struggling families living just blocks away, many of whom faced hunger and isolation, they decided to launch "The Open Table" initiative. This project sought to provide not just meals, but a welcoming environment that embraced the family unit and celebrated diversity in unity.

Every Saturday, tables adorned with vibrant tablecloths and laden with wholesome food dotted the community park. As the sun cast a golden glow upon smiling faces, volunteers prepared to serve with hearts full of compassion. Laughter echoed and stories were shared, weaving connections that transcended socioeconomic barriers. Each plate filled was a message of hope and each shared moment a testament to the relentless pursuit of community and kindness.

The air was fragrant with the aromas of various cuisines—a delicious representation of the cultural tapestry that enveloped the area. Children played freely, their joyous laughter blending with the music of local artists who volunteered their talent to bring more life to the gathering. For many, these Saturdays became a sanctuary of solace, a safe haven where love overflowed, and everyone could dine at one table, side by side, regardless of their previous situations.

The impact of "The Open Table" rippled far beyond the event itself. As relationships blossomed—nurtured by shared meals and authentic conversations—families began to find support among one another. Empowered by their collective experiences, they formed community gardens and educational workshops, pursuing self-sufficiency and resilience together.

Amid this flourishing connection, the church realized the transformative power of their mission work—not only in feeding the hungry but also in feeding the souls yearning for belonging. Each Saturday, they witnessed a miracle: lives changed not just by physical nourishment, but by the camaraderie that Christ exemplified through love and service.

Through this journey of outreach, Grace Community Church discovered that being the Church meant being intimately involved in the fabric of the community—a tangible manifestation of God's grace poured out into the world. They embraced the call to become a beacon of hope, fostering a community where every individual was cherished and empowered.

In embracing the teachings of Jesus, Grace Community Church not only fulfilled its mission but fundamentally reshaped its identity—an embodiment of compassion where all were invited to the table, creating a harmonious symphony of faith, love, and service.

This compelling case study highlights the vibrant impact of mission work within the church community, offering a model for others to follow in their path of service. The story of Grace Community Church reminds us that in every act of kindness, we partake in a divine calling to transform lives and bring about healing within our communities.*

Case Study
True Gospel Tabernacle

Nestled in the heart of South Philadelphia, True Gospel Tabernacle stands as a vibrant testament to the power of faith and community. Under the dedicated leadership of Bishop Ernest McNear, the church has woven a tapestry of compassion and spiritual fervor, becoming a sanctuary for the soul and a beacon of hope for the city's Indonesian immigrant community and beyond. This is the inspiring story of True Gospel Tabernacle, a church that has not only embraced its local neighborhood but has also

---

* **Footnote:** For further exploration of contemporary mission work and its impact, consider reading *"When Helping Hurts: How to Alleviate Poverty Without Hurting the Poor... and Yourself"* by Steve Corbett and Brian Fikkert.

extended its reach across continents, driven by a mission of world evangelization.

A Heart for the Neighbors

The story of True Gospel Tabernacle is a testament to the transformative power of love and acceptance. When thousands of immigrants from Southeast Asia began to arrive in South Philadelphia, the church, led by Bishop McNear, saw an opportunity to embody the teachings of Jesus Christ. Instead of seeing these newcomers as strangers, the church opened its arms, welcoming them with an outpouring of compassion.

In partnership with the Rock Church of Philadelphia, True Gospel Tabernacle shared its facilities and resources, creating a vibrant ministry that bridged cultural and linguistic divides. This partnership not only provided a spiritual home for the Indonesian community but also fostered a sense of unity and purpose among all congregants. It was a living testament to the divine orchestration of having their church location at the very heart of this new community.

Global Vision and Outreach

True Gospel Tabernacle's mission extended far beyond the borders of Philadelphia. Recognizing the global shift of Christianity's center of gravity to the southern hemisphere, Bishop McNear felt a divine calling to engage in international missions. This calling led him to Ghana, where he saw an urgent need for spiritual and physical healing.

In 2003, Bishop McNear organized a trip to Cape Coast, Ghana, as part of a sister-city partnership with Philadelphia. This initiative, which included donating municipal waste disposal trucks, marked the beginning of a deeper engagement with the Ghanaian community. During his visit, Bishop McNear held conferences and training seminars for local pastors, reigniting their passion and vision.

Challenges and Triumphs

The journey was not without its challenges. Bureaucratic hurdles and internal church politics posed significant obstacles. Despite these setbacks, Bishop McNear's unwavering faith and dedication to his mission kept him steadfast. When True Gospel Tabernacle's request to establish a new jurisdiction was initially side-lined, McNear accepted a lesser role, demonstrating humility and resilience. Eventually, under the umbrella of the Church of God in Christ, International, he continued to nurture and expand the church's mission in Ghana.

Innovative Programs and Impact

True Gospel Tabernacle's impact has been multifaceted. In Ghana, one of their most significant contributions has been in the realm of HIV/AIDS education and support. Partnering with Philadelphia FIGHT, a leading organization in HIV/AIDS research and outreach, Bishop McNear spearheaded initiatives to educate and support those affected by the virus. This partnership brought hope and healing to many, breaking the stigma associated with HIV/AIDS and providing much-needed medical and emotional support.

Back home in Philadelphia, the church's daycare program and Christian elementary school offer a nurturing environment for children, aligning with their mission to serve the community holistically. These programs reflect the church's commitment to fostering growth and development, both spiritually and practically.

A Legacy of Faith

The narrative of True Gospel Tabernacle is a powerful reminder of the divine potential within every community. Through the trials and triumphs, the church has remained a steadfast beacon of hope, driven by a profound sense of mission and a deep love for humanity. Bishop Ernest McNear's leadership exemplifies the true spirit of evangelical charismatic Christianity, a faith that is active, compassionate, and transformative.

As True Gospel Tabernacle continues its journey, it stands as a testament to the power of faith in action, a shining example of how a local church can have a global impact. The story of this thriving congregation is a compelling narrative of faith, resilience, and the boundless potential of a community united in love and purpose.*

A PRACTICAL GUIDE TO FULFILLING THE GREAT COMMISSION

The Great Commission, found in Matthew 28:19-20, is a foundational commandment given by Jesus Christ to His disciples. This command is of paramount importance as it encapsulates the mission of the Church: to spread the Gospel, nurture disciples, and teach the teachings of Jesus Christ. It is a divine mandate that calls for action, ensuring that the message of salvation and hope reaches every corner of the earth, transcending time and culture.

Strategies to Fulfill the Great Commission

While the Great Commission may seem like a daunting task, there are practical ways to fulfill this commandment in our everyday lives. Here are some strategies that can help us effectively share the love of Christ and fulfill the mission of the Church:

1. Creating an Effective Evangelism Plan

To spread the Gospel effectively, a structured evangelism plan is essential:

- **Identify the Target Audience:** Understand the

---

* **Footnote:** www.truegospeltabernacle.org

demographics, culture, and needs of the community you aim to reach.
- **Develop Key Messages:** Craft clear and compelling messages that resonate with the target audience, emphasizing the core tenets of the faith.
- **Training Workshops:** Equip church members with the skills and confidence to share their faith through regular training sessions.
- **Outreach Activities:** Organize community events, such as free health clinics, food drives, or educational workshops, to build relationships and open doors for evangelism.
- **Follow-Up Mechanism:** Create a system to follow up with new contacts, providing them with further information and inviting them to church activities.

2. Establishing Effective Small Group Discipleship Programs

Small group discipleship programs foster deeper connections and spiritual growth:

- **Group Formation:** Organize small groups based on shared interests, life stages, or geographical locations.
- **Curriculum Development:** Choose or create study materials that align with the church's theological stance and goals.

- **Training Facilitators:** Identify and train dedicated leaders who can guide discussions and support group members.
- **Regular Meetings:** Schedule consistent meeting times and create a welcoming environment for open and honest conversations.
- **Service Projects:** Encourage groups to participate in community service, reflecting the love of Christ through practical acts of kindness.

3. Empowering and Training Volunteers to Engage in Outreach

Volunteers play a crucial role in outreach efforts:

- **Recruitment Drives:** Host events to recruit volunteers from within the church and the broader community.
- **Orientation Programs:** Provide comprehensive training sessions that cover the mission, vision, and practical aspects of outreach activities.
- **Mentorship:** Pair new volunteers with experienced mentors to guide them and foster a sense of belonging.
- **Regular Feedback:** Conduct regular feedback sessions to address challenges and celebrate successes.
- **Recognition:** Acknowledge and celebrate the

contributions of volunteers through appreciation events and awards.

4. Creating an Online Platform to Reach a Wider Audience

An online platform expands the church's reach:

- **Website Development:** Build a user-friendly website that offers information about the church, its beliefs, and upcoming events.
- **Content Creation:** Regularly post sermons, articles, and testimonies that inspire and educate visitors.
- **Social Media Integration:** Utilize social media channels to promote content and engage with a broader audience.
- **Online Community:** Create forums or groups where individuals can ask questions, share experiences, and receive support.
- **Live Streaming:** Offer live streaming of services and events to reach those who cannot attend in person.

5. Developing Partnerships with Other Organizations or Churches

Partnerships amplify efforts and resources:

- **Identify Potential Partners:** Look for organizations or churches with similar missions and values.
- **Collaborative Projects:** Develop joint initiatives that address community needs, such as food distribution or educational programs.
- **Resource Sharing:** Pool resources, such as volunteers, funding, and facilities, to maximize impact.
- **Regular Communication:** Maintain open lines of communication to coordinate efforts and share successes.
- **Mutual Support:** Offer and receive support through prayer, encouragement, and shared experiences.

6. Utilizing Social Media Tools to Spread the Word

Social media is a powerful tool for outreach:

- **Platform Selection:** Choose platforms that best reach your target audience, such as Facebook, Instagram, or Twitter.
- **Regular Posting:** Maintain a consistent posting schedule with diverse content, including inspirational quotes, event promotions, and community stories.
- **Engagement:** Actively engage with followers by responding to comments, messages, and participating in discussions.

- **Advertising:** Use paid advertising to target specific demographics and increase visibility.
- **Analytics:** Monitor social media analytics to understand what content resonates and adjust strategies accordingly.

7. Organizing Community Outreach Events

Community events build bridges and foster relationships:

- **Event Planning:** Identify the needs of the community and plan events that address those needs, such as health fairs, job training workshops, or cultural festivals.
- **Promotion:** Promote events through flyers, social media, and partnerships with local organizations.
- **Volunteer Coordination:** Mobilize volunteers to assist with event setup, execution, and follow-up.
- **Engagement Activities:** Incorporate activities that encourage interaction and relationship-building, such as games, discussions, and shared meals.
- **Follow-Up:** Collect contact information and follow up with attendees to invite them to future events and church services.

8. Integrating the Great Commission into Existing Church Programs

Incorporating the Great Commission into all church activities ensures a consistent focus on mission:

- **Sermon Series:** Preach regularly on the importance of the Great Commission and practical ways to fulfill it.
- **Children and Youth Programs:** Integrate mission-focused lessons and activities into programs for younger members.
- **Adult Education:** Offer classes and workshops that equip members with the knowledge and skills to share their faith effectively.
- **Prayer Initiatives:** Organize prayer groups that focus on interceding for mission efforts and specific outreach opportunities.
- **Mission Trips:** Plan short-term mission trips to provide hands-on experience in evangelism and service.

Monitoring Progress and Tracking Impact

To ensure the effectiveness of these strategies, it is crucial to monitor progress and track impact:

- **Set Clear Goals:** Establish specific, measurable, achievable, relevant, and time-bound (SMART) goals for each strategy.

- **Regular Evaluation:** Conduct regular evaluations to assess progress towards goals and identify areas for improvement.
- **Feedback Mechanisms:** Implement feedback mechanisms, such as surveys or focus groups, to gather input from participants and the community.
- **Impact Reporting:** Create reports that highlight successes, challenges, and lessons learned, and share them with the congregation and stakeholders.
- **Continuous Improvement:** Use the insights gained from monitoring and evaluation to refine strategies and enhance future efforts.

In conclusion, fulfilling the Great Commission requires a comprehensive and multifaceted approach. By implementing these strategies with dedication and compassion, we can effectively spread the message of Christ's love and build a community that reflects the divine purpose of the Gospel and fosters a sense of belonging for all.

The Great Commission remains a living mandate for today's Christian community. It calls us to engage with the world, sharing the message of Christ and making disciples. By understanding its historical context, theological significance, and practical applications, we can continue Jesus' mission with renewed passion and purpose.

Whether you're a church leader, theologian, or individual believer, we all have a role to play in fulfilling the Great Commission. Let's commit to prayer, equip ourselves and others, and work together to spread the Gospel and transform lives.

FORGING KINGDOM CONNECTIONS

BUILDING PARTNERSHIPS FOR LASTING IMPACTS

Have you ever wondered how strategic partnerships can impact your business or organization? In the Bible, partnerships played a crucial role in achieving God's work, demonstrating the power of alliances rooted in faith and purpose. This blog post explores biblical examples of strategic partnerships, offering valuable insights for modern-day Christian businesses and organizations. By understanding these principles, you can forge connections that not only enhance your mission but also align with God's plan.

UNDERSTANDING STRATEGIC PARTNERSHIPS IN SCRIPTURE

Both the Old and New Testaments offer a wealth of examples of remarkable alliances, illustrating how individuals and communities united to pursue common goals. From the covenants established between God and His people to the collaborations among disciples and early Christians, these alliances underscore the significance of unity, faith, and cooperation in overcoming challenges and fulfilling divine purposes throughout history.

The Old Testament is filled with compelling examples of powerful alliances that highlight the significance of relationships in attaining remarkable outcomes. Take, for instance, the bond between David and Jonathan. Their friendship was more than just personal; it was a strategic alliance that helped David navigate the treacherous political landscape of Saul's court. Jonathan's loyalty and willingness to protect David played a crucial role in David's survival, ultimately enabling him to rise to the throne of Israel (1 Samuel 18-20). Similarly, Ruth and Naomi's partnership showcases profound loyalty and mutual support in a time of adversity. Ruth's determination to stay with Naomi, despite the loss of their husbands, led to her marriage to Boaz, which not only secured her future but also ensured the continuation of Naomi's family line and fulfillment of God's promises (Ruth 1-4).

The New Testament also highlights the significance of partnerships in spreading the Gospel message. Paul's missionary journeys were successful due to his collaborations with various companions, including Barnabas, Silas, and Timothy. Each of these partnerships brought unique strengths and perspectives, allowing them to navigate different cultural landscapes and effectively communicate the Gospel's transformative message. Their alliances enabled the spread of the Gospel across diverse regions, from the bustling cities of Asia Minor to the heart of the Roman Empire, demonstrating the strength that comes from working together for a common cause (Acts 13-20).

These scriptural examples reveal that partnerships are not just beneficial but essential for fulfilling God's work. Through alliances, individuals can leverage each other's strengths, provide mutual support, and achieve a greater impact than they could alone. This principle is as relevant today as it was in biblical times, reminding us that collaboration can lead to extraordinary outcomes in our personal and spiritual journeys. In today's world, where challenges can feel overwhelming, forming meaningful partnerships can provide the encouragement and collective strength necessary to make a difference, both in our communities and beyond.

LESSONS FOR CHRISTIAN BUSINESSES AND ORGANIZATIONS

As we consider the examples of partnerships in Scripture, there are valuable lessons that Christian businesses and organizations can apply to their own pursuits. Here are a few key takeaways:

How can these ancient partnerships inform modern-day business practices? First, they teach us the importance of shared values. Just as David and Jonathan's friendship was founded on mutual respect and unwavering faith in God, your business partnerships should not only align with your core values and mission but also foster a deep sense of trust and loyalty. This alignment creates a strong foundation that allows for collaboration and innovation, enabling partners to navigate challenges together while remaining committed to their shared goals.

Effective collaboration is another key lesson drawn from biblical examples. Paul's remarkable success in spreading the Gospel was due in part to his ability to work harmoniously with a diverse group of individuals, each contributing their unique strengths. In today's context, this means fostering open communication, mutual respect, and a shared vision among partners. Encouraging an environment where all voices are heard can lead to creative solutions and a stronger team dynamic. These elements are crucial for any successful partnership, as they not only enhance productivity but also build lasting relationships that can withstand the test of time.

By applying these biblical principles, Christian businesses and organizations can create partnerships that not only further their individual missions but also contribute to the broader goal of advancing God's kingdom. This holistic approach ensures that your work has both immediate and eternal impact. It encourages businesses to think beyond profit margins and consider the positive influence they can have on their communities and the world at large. By integrating faith-based values into their operational strategies, organizations can inspire others and create a ripple effect of goodness that transcends their immediate reach.

CASE STUDIES AND TESTIMONIALS

To further illustrate the power of partnerships in Christian businesses and organizations, let's take a look at some real-life examples:

The Bible Project & YouVersion Bible App

One notable example of a successful strategic partnership is between The Bible Project and the YouVersion Bible App. The Bible Project, known for its innovative visual storytelling through animated videos and educational resources, brings Scripture to life in a way that resonates with a diverse audience. This creative approach, combined with YouVersion's extensive global reach and user-friendly interface, has made engaging with the Bible more accessible than ever before.

By integrating The Bible Project's content into the YouVersion app, users are provided with rich, contextual insights that enhance their understanding of the Scriptures. This partnership has resulted in millions of new users interacting with the Bible daily, demonstrating the profound impact of collaboration in spreading God's word. Together, these organizations are not only transforming how individuals engage with their faith but are also fostering a vibrant community of learners and seekers around the world.

Gospel for Asia & K.P. Yohannan Ministries

Another inspiring testimonial comes from the impactful partnership between Gospel for Asia and K.P. Yohannan Ministries. This collaboration has not only significantly increased support and visibility for their mission to bring hope and Christ's love to the most unreached populations in Asia, but it has also created a network of resources and volunteers dedicated to this cause.

The 10/40 Window represents a crucial geographic region, spanning from 10 degrees to 40 degrees north latitude and encompassing countries in North Africa, the Middle East, and Asia. This area is home to a significant portion of the world's unreached people, where the need for the eternal message of the Gospel is both urgent and profound. As we reflect on the call to bring the light of Christ to these regions, we are reminded of the compassion and love that Jesus embodied, urging us to step beyond our comfort zones and engage with those who have yet to hear His message.

Partnerships formed with local believers and organizations like Gospel for Asia are essential in this endeavor. By working collaboratively with those who understand the culture and context, we can foster genuine connections and share the Gospel authentically. Additionally, leveraging technology and resources can amplify our reach, making it possible to deliver His message to remote areas where traditional outreach methods may fall short. In this mission, it is essential to approach with a heart full of grace, humility, and respect, understanding that every conversation holds the potential to plant seeds of faith that can blossom into lasting generational change. Together, let us rise to this sacred challenge—carrying the message of hope and redemption into the depths of the 10/40 Window, believing that even the smallest efforts are valuable in the pursuit of the Great Commission.

World Vision & The Global Leadership Summit

World Vision's collaboration with The Global Leadership Summit stands as a remarkable example of effective partnership in action. By engaging Christian leaders from various backgrounds and communities through the summit, they not only increased support for vital global development programs but also fostered a shared vision for community transformation that resonates deeply with participants. This partnership highlights the immense potential for long-term, positive change when organizations unite their efforts and resources. By leveraging the strengths and insights of diverse leaders, they are able to address pressing issues facing communities worldwide more effectively, ultimately working towards a brighter future for all. Through initiatives stemming from this collaboration, meaningful progress can be made in areas such as education, health, and poverty alleviation, demonstrating the power of collective action in driving sustainable development.

PRACTICAL STEPS FOR FORMING AND NURTURING STRATEGIC PARTNERSHIPS

As we reflect on these inspirational partnerships, it's essential to consider how we can apply the same principles in our own businesses and organizations. Here are some practical steps for forming and nurturing strategic partnerships:

The first step in forming a strategic partnership is identifying suitable partners. To effectively further the Great Commission through strategic partnerships, consider the following approaches for identifying suitable partners:

- **Shared Vision and Values**: Seek organizations that have a commitment to spreading the Gospel and embody similar faith-based principles. Aligning on values ensures a strong foundation for collaboration.
- **Community Needs Assessment**: Conduct research to understand the specific needs within communities you aim to serve. Identify organizations already making an impact in those areas, as they can offer valuable insights and resources.
- **Networking within Faith Communities**: Engage with local churches, fellowships, and Christian networks to discover potential partners. These relationships often yield fruitful collaborations grounded in mutual trust.

- **Utilizing Social Media and Online Platforms**: Leverage platforms like LinkedIn and Facebook to connect with like-minded organizations and individuals who share your mission. Online communities can be a powerful resource for partnership opportunities.
- **Attending Conferences and Events**: Participate in Christian conferences, seminars, and community events focused on mission work. These gatherings provide avenues for meeting potential partners and sharing visions for impactful collaboration.
- **Exploring Inter-denominational Networks**: Cultivate relationships with organizations from various denominations. This diversity can enrich partnerships, bringing in a wealth of experience and innovative ideas to reach broader audiences.
- **Evaluating Existing Partnerships**: Look within your network for organizations that may already be collaborating but not fully engaging. Reinvigorating these relationships can lead to renewed efforts and expanded reach in the mission field.

Look for organizations that share your values, mission, and vision. Conduct thorough research and engage in conversations to ensure alignment.

BUILDING STRONG RELATIONSHIPS

Once you've identified potential partners, focus on building strong, enduring relationships. Building strong, enduring relationships is a sacred process that requires intentionality, openness, and love. To begin this journey of connection, one must first approach each interaction with a heart aligned with compassion and understanding. Here are some ways to initiate the building of these invaluable relationships:

- **Active Listening**: Embrace the art of listening deeply. When engaging with potential partners, show genuine interest in their thoughts, feelings, and experiences. By valuing their perspectives, you create a space where trust can flourish.
- **Shared Purpose**: Articulate a clear, shared purpose that resonates with both parties. Together, explore how your visions align and how collaboration can amplify your efforts to serve others. This alignment fosters a sense of unity and commitment towards a common goal.
- **Open Communication**: Establish transparent communication from the outset. Encourage open dialogues where both partners feel safe to express their ideas and concerns. Regular check-ins and feedback loops can strengthen this foundation.

- **Mutual Support**: Engage in acts of support that demonstrate your commitment to one another's success. Celebrate each other's achievements, offer resources, and create opportunities for mutual growth within the partnership.
- **Cultural Sensitivity**: Approach your partnership with a spirit of learning and respect for different cultures and practices. Recognizing and honoring diversity enriches relationships and fosters a deeper understanding of one another.
- **Regular Engagement**: Schedule regular meetings or activities to maintain an ongoing connection. Whether through virtual calls or in-person gatherings, consistent engagement helps to solidify the bond and keeps the momentum of the partnership alive.
- **Prayerful Reflection**: Lastly, incorporate prayer and spiritual reflection into your partnership. Seeking divine guidance together can deepen your commitment and provide clarity as you navigate challenges and opportunities.

By nurturing these principles, individuals can cultivate relationships that not only endure but also thrive as beacons of hope and transformation within their communities. Let us remember that every meaningful partnership is a call to serve together, strengthening the impact of our collective mission.

Invest time in getting to know your partners, understanding their goals, and finding common ground. This foundation is crucial for a successful partnership.

MAINTAINING INTEGRITY

Finally, maintaining the integrity of your partnerships is essential for long-term success and alignment with your mission. It is important to ensure that your alliances not only align with biblical teachings but also actively promote and uphold your core values in every interaction. Take the time to assess the compatibility of your partnerships regularly, considering factors such as ethical practices, shared goals, and mutual respect. This ongoing evaluation will help you determine whether they continue to serve your mission effectively and contribute to fulfilling God's purpose in your endeavors. Engaging in open and honest communication with your partners can also strengthen these relationships and foster a deeper commitment to shared values.

A WORD ABOUT LOYALTY IN PARTNERSHIPS

Loyalty is the result of a steadfast commitment that we cultivate in our partnerships, a divine thread that binds us together in our shared mission. In the spirit of collaboration, we are reminded of the profound truth in Proverbs 17:17:

> *"A friend loves at all times, and a brother is born for a time of adversity."*

This scripture encapsulates the essence of loyalty—standing by one another through challenges and triumphs alike, embodying the love that Christ exemplified in His relationships.

Loyalty nurtures trust, fosters resilience, and fortifies our willingness to persevere even when faced with trials. As we embark on this journey of partnership, let us echo the words of Ecclesiastes 4:9-10:

> *"Two are better than one, because they have a good return for their labour: If either of them falls down, one can help the other up."*

In our unwavering loyalty to one another, we create an environment where we can support and uplift each other, leading to greater impact and fulfillment of our divine purpose.

Let us commit ourselves to embodying loyalty as a sacred promise, knowing that it is through these bonds that we can truly reflect God's love and grace in the world. As we honor our commitments and uphold the integrity of our relationships, we become instruments of divine unity, empowering one another to shine brightly in our collective calling.

THE FUTURE OF STRATEGIC PARTNERSHIPS IN THE CHRISTIAN COMMUNITY

Christian partnerships are indeed here to stay, a powerful testament to the divine orchestration at work within our communities. In this time of incredible opportunity, let us seize the moment to leverage these alliances for the greater glory of the Kingdom. Each partnership, rooted in faith and purpose, has the potential to be a force for transformation, extending far beyond our individual capabilities.

The landscape of faith-based collaborations is continually evolving, driven by the rapid advancements in technology and communication. These developments have opened up a wealth of opportunities for Christian businesses and organizations to form strategic partnerships that can amplify their impact. As digital platforms become more accessible, there is an increasing ability to connect with like-minded individuals and groups across the globe. This interconnectedness allows for the sharing of resources, ideas, and best practices, fostering innovative approaches to address community needs. Moreover, the rise of social media and collaborative tools enables organizations to engage in meaningful dialogue, build relationships, and create synergies that further their missions. In this dynamic environment, the potential for faith-based collaborations to thrive and make a significant difference has never been greater.

In the broad landscape of business and faith, the opportunity to network with like-minded companies offers a profound chance to forge connections that align with our shared mission. Engaging with networking groups like **Kingdom Business Network** (www.kingdombusinessnetwork.com) opens doors to a community that is committed to aligning business practices with Kingdom principles. This network serves as a sanctuary for those who desire to cultivate relationships grounded in faith and purpose, fostering an environment where collaboration and innovation can flourish.

As we **connect**, **grow**, and **fund** the Great Commission together, we empower one another to extend the reach of our collective impact. Each partnership within the Kingdom Business Network is a stepping stone towards fulfilling God's calling in the marketplace, allowing us to pool resources, share insights, and support each other's missions. By joining forces in this manner, we not only amplify our efforts but also become beacons of hope and transformation in our communities. Let us embrace the power of unity, recognizing that together, we can achieve great things, fulfilling the divine mandate to spread love, compassion, and the Gospel to all corners of the earth.

However, as we explore these new opportunities, it's crucial to stay true to our faith and the teachings of the Bible. This means not only adhering to the core tenets of our beliefs but also reflecting those principles in our daily interactions and decision-making processes. By grounding our partnerships in biblical principles, we can ensure that our work remains aligned with God's will, fostering an environment of integrity and purpose. When we prioritize faith in our endeavors, we are more likely to cultivate meaningful relationships that honor the teachings of the Bible and our commitment to Christian values while contributing positively to the communities we serve. Embracing this approach allows us to navigate challenges with a steadfast spirit and encourages others to join us in our mission.

In conclusion, Strategic partnerships have always played a vital role in achieving God's work, both in biblical times and in our contemporary world. Throughout history, we see examples of individuals and communities coming together to fulfill a greater purpose, whether it was in the early church or through modern-day ministries. By understanding and applying these principles of collaboration and mutual support, Christian businesses and organizations can forge meaningful connections that not only enhance their mission but also further God's kingdom in impactful ways. These partnerships can lead to innovative solutions to challenges, shared resources, and a unified effort toward serving the community. Ultimately, when Christians work together in partnership, they create a lasting impact that resonates far beyond their immediate goals, embodying the essence of service and love that Christ taught us.

MAY I INTRODUCE YOU TO JESUS?

DISCOVERING THE LIFE CHANGING JOY OF LIVING FOR JESUS

Are you feeling lost, searching for a purpose in life? Do you feel that something is missing, and you are not sure what it is? Do you want to know more about Jesus and the Bible? If yes, then you are in the right place. In this chapter, we will explore what a relationship with Jesus can mean for your life and eternity. The Bible says that when we come to Jesus, we receive spiritual rebirth, the forgiveness of sins, and eternal life. Let's talk about it.

The Biblical Basis for Coming to Jesus

God has provided us with precise instructions on how to come to Him through His Word, the Bible. Our first step is acknowledging our sins. Romans 3:23 says,

"For all have sinned and fall short of the glory of God."

Therefore, we must recognize that we cannot save ourselves with our own efforts. However, Jesus can save us, and we must believe in Him to receive salvation.

Acceptance and belief in His Word affect our lives in many ways. John 1:12 says,

> *"Yet to all who did receive him, to those who believed in his name, he gave the right to become children of God."*

By accepting Jesus into our lives, we gain the privilege of being God's children, and this changes our identity. We will have a new purpose in life and a new perspective on our struggles. We will experience forgiveness, acceptance, divine love, and the joy of living for God daily.

The Cross of Calvary reveals the ultimate sacrifice of Jesus Christ for our sins. Romans 5:8 says,

> *"But God demonstrates his love for us in this: While we were still sinners, Christ died for us."*

Jesus paid the price for our sins, and we can receive forgiveness and salvation through Him. It is through His death and resurrection that we can come to the Father and receive the Holy Spirit.

As humans, we all have our shortcomings and faults. No one is perfect, and that's why we need Jesus in our lives. Romans 6:23 states that the penalty for sin is death, but through Jesus, we have the opportunity to receive the gift of eternal life. It's a beautiful thing to know that there's a way out of the darkness, and that's through Jesus

Christ. It's not an easy decision to make, but it's a crucial one that we all must make if we want to experience true freedom and life. So, if you're feeling lost and hopeless today, know that there's hope in Jesus. He's waiting with open arms to welcome you home!

Praying a prayer of salvation is a simple and powerful step toward salvation. We must confess our faith and ask for forgiveness of our sins. Romans 10:9 says,

> *"If you declare with your mouth, "Jesus is Lord," and believe in your heart that God raised him from the dead, you will be saved."*

Here is a simple guide:

DEAR LORD JESUS,

> *I know that I am a sinner and that I cannot save myself. I believe that you died on the Cross for my sins and that you rose again. Please forgive me of my sins and come into my heart. Right now, I confess and receive You as my Lord and Savior. Thank you for giving me eternal life. In Jesus' name, Amen.*

Congratulations on your decision to follow Christ and join the family of God! You are no longer alone in your journey of faith. It's exciting to think about the wonderful things God has in store for you as you grow and mature in Him. Whether you are new to Christianity or have walked with the Lord for a while, this guide will help you navigate the ups and downs of your faith journey.

Being a part of the Family of God is a rich and rewarding experience that comes with responsibilities and opportunities. Now that you have received salvation, you have the privilege of being called a child of God. The concept of having a personal relationship with Jesus Christ must be taken seriously, as it is an ongoing process if one is to continuously grow in their faith.

Daily Prayer

The first step is to understand the power of prayer. Prayer is a conversation with God that helps establish and strengthen an intimate relationship with Him. Cultivate the habit of prayer by setting aside a specific time each day to talk with God. One of the most important components of prayer is learning how to listen to what God is trying to say. Many people think that prayer is constantly talking to God. May I encourage you that prayer is one part talking and two parts listening. Just look in the mirror; we all have one mouth and two ears.

Praying daily is a wonderful way to connect with God's heart and deepen your relationship with Him. It allows for open communication so that you can share your thoughts, feelings, and aspirations with Him. You may also take this time to thank Him for your blessings and ask for His guidance in making decisions. With each prayer, you build a stronger connection with God and can find peace knowing that He is always there to listen and support you.

Throughout the years, many people have asked me, "How can I hear God's voice?" My answer to them has consistently been,

"If we sit in God's presence, we can learn His voice."

God speaks to everyone differently. He wants to have an active relationship with you, and the best way to do this is through communication. One of the ways that God has communicated to us is through His Word.

Daily Bible Reading

Reading the Bible is an incredible way to receive guidance on God's will for your life. The Bible contains gems of wisdom and encouragement that can help us navigate the twists and turns of life. Whether we're facing a tough decision, feeling lost or simply seeking direction, the Bible is a faithful companion that provides solid, reliable advice. What's more, the Bible is a gift that strengthens our relationship with God. Through reading its pages, we can learn about His character, understand His love and gain a deeper appreciation of His goodness. Reading the Bible isn't just about finding direction - it's about drawing closer to the One who created us and has a hope-filled plan for our lives.

To grow in faith and knowledge, one must engage in daily bible reading and study. The Bible is the guidebook that reveals who God is, what He has done, and what He expects of us. In addition to personal bible reading, it's important to receive sound teaching through fellowship with other believers. It's helpful to attend small groups, Sunday sermons, or listen to online messages. With practice, the things you learn will become deeply rooted in your heart and transform your life.

Christian Friends

Finding Christian friends is also essential to your growth in faith. When you're immersed in a community of believers, you have the opportunity to build deep, authentic relationships. These relationships build support and accountability, which will help you stay on the right path. Connecting with a church community is vital to your spiritual growth. A church provides a place where you can worship God in community, hear the Word preached, and serve the body of Christ.

Being part of a church provides not only solid teaching but a community of like-minded believers that share a common faith. There is nothing quite like experiencing the joy of fellowship with others who are seeking to grow in their relationship with God. You'll find people who come from all walks of life, with different backgrounds and experiences but united in a common goal - to know and love God more deeply. As you sit under the teaching of pastors and teachers, you'll discover a depth to your faith that you never thought possible. Through worship, prayer, and study of the

Bible, you'll feel your heart expanding with an overwhelming sense of gratitude and thankfulness for all that God is doing in your life. Truly, belonging to a church is an experience that is both fulfilling and life changing.

Developing a Servants Heart

Putting your learning into practice through the practical application of your faith is an important step in growth. Serving others is one way to do so. Jesus spent His life serving others and has called us to do the same. Jesus' example reminds us that we need to get outside of our comfort zones and bless others with our time, energy, and resources. Volunteer at church, donate to a charity, or work in your community. With time, as you serve and bless others, you'll find that God is guiding and shaping you into a better version of yourself.

Living Grateful

Living a life that is grateful, faithful, and holy is truly a blessing. As we honor God in all areas of our lives, we can't help but feel an overwhelming sense of joy and fulfillment. It's not always the easiest path to take, but when we choose to put our trust in Him and seek His will for our lives, we can rest assured that we are on the right track. When we live with gratitude in our hearts, we begin to see the world in a different light, and our relationships with others are strengthened. Ultimately, living a life that honors God is the best decision we can make, and we can trust that He will guide us every step of the way.

Pride and gratitude cannot co-exist. Rejoicing in the blessings of salvation is the ultimate goal of every Christian. It's easy to get bogged down in day-to-day challenges that we forget to celebrate the victory we have in Jesus. To celebrate the goodness of God, it's essential to practice gratitude. Remember that your salvation is a free gift from God that you didn't deserve, and nothing you do can take it away. Celebrate divine love, mercy, and grace by sharing joyful testimonies with others. Encourage others with your story and how God has changed your life.

Welcome to the Family!

ABOUT THE AUTHOR

For more information on Dr. Jonathan Vorce just go to
www.about.me/jonathanvorce

Affordable | Accessible | Accredited | Online

Dr. Vorce is the Chancellor of Covenant University, Inc. Degrees range from first year through Ph.D.

More information is available on our website:
www.covenantuniversityonline.com

ALSO BY JONATHAN VORCE

Presence Driven
Hosting the Holy Ghost
Christian Leadership
Building Successful Ministry
Shepherding in the 21st Century
Kingdom Economics
Divine Authority
The Ministry of Presence (Chaplaincy)
Non-Profit Creation and Management
Angels Among Us
10 Keys to God's Miracle Working Power

All books may be ordered on Amazon.com and most online places where books are sold.

www.ingramcontent.com/pod-product-compliance
Lightning Source LLC
Chambersburg PA
CBHW052251220526
45471CB00001B/292